HARLEY-DAVIDSON
THE COMPLETE HISTORY

HARLEY-DAVIDSON

THE COMPLETE HISTORY

DARWIN HOLMSTROM, EDITOR

Quarto is the authority on a wide range of topics.

Quarto educates, entertains and enriches the lives of our readers—enthusiasts and lovers of hands-on living.

www.quartoknows.com

First published in 2016 by Motorbooks, an imprint of Quarto Publishing Group USA Inc., 400 First Avenue North, Suite 400, Minneapolis, MN 55401 USA. Telephone: (612) 344-8100 Fax: (612) 344-8692

quartoknows.com

Visit our blogs at quartoknows.com

Motorbooks titles are also available at discounts in bulk quantity for industrial or sales-promotional use. For details contact the Special Sales Manager at Quarto Publishing Group USA Inc., 400 First Avenue North, Suite 400, Minneapolis, MN 55401 USA.

10 9 8 7 6 5 4 3 2 1

ISBN: 978-0-7603-5000-3

Acquiring Editor: Darwin Holmstrom
Project Manager: Jordan Wiklund
Art Director: Brad Springer
Cover and layout design: Simon Larkin

Printed in China

CONTENTS

THE *A PRIORI* MOTORCYCLE

BY DARWIN HOLMSTROM

> "*WE HAVE IN OUR MINDS AN* A PRIORI *MOTORCYCLE WHICH HAS CONTINUITY IN TIME AND SPACE.*"
> —Robert M. Pirsig, *Zen and the Art of Motorcycle Maintenance*

When most people close their eyes and imagine a motorcycle, chances are that motorcycle looks very much like a Harley-Davidson. That happens not just because Harleys are the most popular bikes in America, or because the H-D marketing folks are geniuses at what they do. That happens because Harley-Davidson builds the archetypal motorcycle, the mythic bike that exists beyond the input provided by our traditional senses.

The philosopher Kant called such mythic archetypes *a priori* knowledge—knowledge we can't learn, only intuit. This knowledge speaks to us in feelings, not words, just like Harley-Davidson motorcycles. The Motor Company builds motorcycles that look the way the primordial biker inside each of us feels motorcycles should look.

When I close my eyes, my inner biker flashes an image of a 1963 XLCH Sportster through my mind, and damned if I don't lust after a mid-1960s XLCH Sportster. This desire makes little sense from any logical standpoint, and people often try to talk me out of buying such a beast. They regale me with cautionary tales of magneto ignitions gone awry. They fill my head with horror stories of the shattered ankles that can result from poorly timed kick starts. They warn me of rear cylinders blown apart so hard that shrapnel explodes from the cases with enough force to lacerate the toughest engineer's boot.

In truth, a 1963 XLCH Sportster would not meet my present needs very well. I use a motorcycle for three primary purposes: commuting, touring, and sport riding. For commuting, a modern Evolution Sportster would prove much more practical than a temperamental classic like the XLCH. For touring I'd be better off with any version of the Twin Cam Electra Glide. And for spirited riding I tend to prefer high-performance European sportbikes, bikes capable of arcing through corners at three times the posted speed limit. All these motorcycles would be more logical choices than a mid-1960s Sportster, but when I close my eyes, it is not the latest Ducati, Electra Ultra Glide Classic, or even current Sportster that pops up on my internal radar. It's a 1963 XLCH.

There is, I think, a reason Harley-Davidson motorcycles define the very word *motorcycle* for so many people. The primordial biker inside each of us doesn't think about things like torsional stiffness, mass centralization, or maximum power-to-weight ratios. The primordial biker thinks about motorcycles at a much more elemental level. And what could be more elemental than a Harley-Davidson motorcycle? A big, powerful engine (V-twin, of course), a couple of wheels, a place to put some fuel, a place to sit, a simple frame to tie it all together: You put those basic pieces together, you come up with an XLCH Sportster. What more do you need?

We all receive slightly different mythic input on what constitutes the archetypal motorcycle. Steve Anderson's inner biker may tell him the XLCR Café Racer is the *a priori* motorcycle. Dain Gingerelli might picture an elemental chopper or bobber. Allan Girdler may envision an XR750 dirt tracker, and Greg Field would almost certainly conjure up a 1936 Knucklehead. Others may see a Heritage Softail, a Road King, or a Dyna Wide Glide as displaying the essence of the motorcycle. They may even consider the current Sportster series or the 1963 XLCH Sportster that defines the notion of *motorcycle* deep within my own reptilian brain stem.

Perhaps therein lies the reason that Harley-Davidson motorcycles continue to dominate our very perceptions of what a motorcycle is—they have a continuity in time and space that locates us. They provide fixed stars that anchor us, provide us with some stability in this ever-changing chaotic world. That continuity is, after all, what Robert M. Pirsig described as the definition of the *a priori* motorcycle.

The editor's *a priori* motorcycle: a 1963 XLCH. *David Blattel*

CHAPTER 1

THE EARLY YEARS

BY HERBERT WAGNER

Lieut. John Greenway.

NOW AND THEN I'LL RUN INTO SOMEONE WHO ASKS IF THE GHOST OF HARLEY OR DAVIDSON WANDERS THE OLD RED BRICK FACTORY ON JUNEAU AVENUE. THE PLACE IS OLD ENOUGH FOR GHOSTS. THE FIRST 1910 PORTION WENT UP NEXT TO THE LONG-VANISHED 1906–1909 WOOD AND BRICK PLANT, RIGHT UP THE BLOCK FROM THE OLD WOODSHED BEHIND THE DAVIDSON FAMILY RESIDENCE. IF A GHOST EXISTS, IT CERTAINLY FEELS AT HOME. AND DOESN'T THE OLD HARLEY-DAVIDSON NICKNAME "SILENT GRAY FELLOW" INVOKE A PHANTOM THAT HAUNTS THE MIDNIGHT HIGHWAY?

ABOVE: During World War I, Harley-Davidson motorcycles went from being pleasure machines to war vehicles. Many were sold to the British government. Seen here is John Greenway of the British army on a 1915 three-speed model with pedal starting.

Ghosts aside, the spirit of Harley-Davidson's founders still inhabits the old factory in an inspirational sense. Stroll around its red brick walls sometime and you'll know what I mean.

The early years of Harley-Davidson involve ghosts and dreams. Of people and bikes long vanished, people who created and raised the Harley-Davidson motorcycle above all others, leaving in their wake memories, mysteries, and legends.

THE ORIGIN

Relaying a true and factual accounting of Harley-Davidson's origins presents a challenge. After 1908, the Motor Company began veering from the facts for marketing purposes. Specifically, the build dates of the first two motorcycles constructed by Harley and

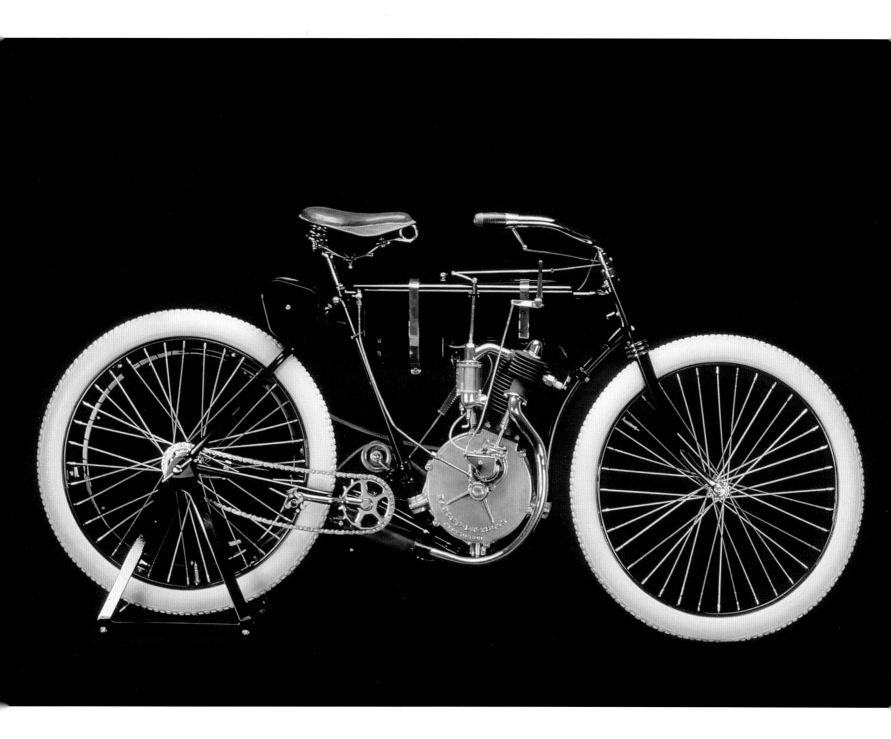

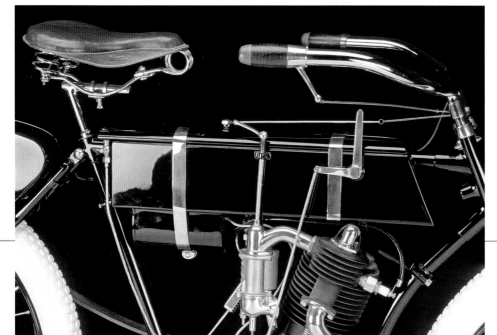

ABOVE: Every journey must start somewhere, and Harley-Davidson's began with this motorcycle, the 1903 serial number 1.

LEFT: Simple-yet-intricate linkage controls served as the primary connection between the rider and the first Harley-Davidson engine.

ABOVE: The 1905 single-cylinder engine was an inlet-over-exhaust (F-head) design, state of the art at the time. The engine displaced 27 cubic inches.

BELOW: The 1905 Model 1 had a three-coil seat for rider comfort. Unofficial records show total production amounted to five bikes, priced at $200 each.

Davidson—two totally different designs—were confused, and their respective identities sometimes merged into a single machine.

The founders were too busy building and selling motorcycles to accurately record their early experiences. In 1942, Arthur Davidson recalled the origin of Harley-Davidson: "It just growed . . . like Topsy . . . with luck." But it wasn't just luck.

In America, the notion of a gasoline-powered bicycle had been kicked around like a carnival freak since the early 1890s, when the shady capitalist-inventor Edward Joel Pennington promoted his latest device, "the Motor Cycle." In 1895, Pennington demonstrated his gasoline-powered two-wheeler on Milwaukee's Wisconsin Avenue. Onlookers mobbed the scene, including, one might speculate, two fourteen-year-old chums, named William S. (Bill) Harley and Arthur (Art) Davidson, living in that neighborhood. Pennington's impractical but mesmerizing invention may have inspired the notion of the motorcycle in the minds of these two boys.

The motorcycle remained a wishing-well fantasy until the lightweight, reliable de Dion-Bouton-type engine arrived from France in the late 1890s. In 1901 the first motorcycles appeared in Milwaukee. That July, twenty-year-old Bill Harley drew plans for a "bicycle motor," plans that in part survive in the Harley family today. Harley's 1901 bicycle motor was about the size of a large chainsaw engine (7.07 cubic inches/106cc). According to legend, a "German draughtsman" gave Harley some engine construction tips, then vanished into history without a trace.

BELOW: Then, as now, early Harleys had belt final drives. However, those first belts were made of leather, not the composite belts used today.

ABOVE: Horsepower for the 1905 Model 1 was rated at 3.25, enough to help racer Perry E. Mack set a new speed record at his local track.

BELOW: Harley-Davidson Motor Company president Walter Davidson seen at the time of his famous 1000 plus 5 point Diamond Medal win in the prestigious New York State endurance contest held in 1908. Walter's big win firmly put H-D on the national motorcycle map and made the firm a main competitor to industry leader Indian.

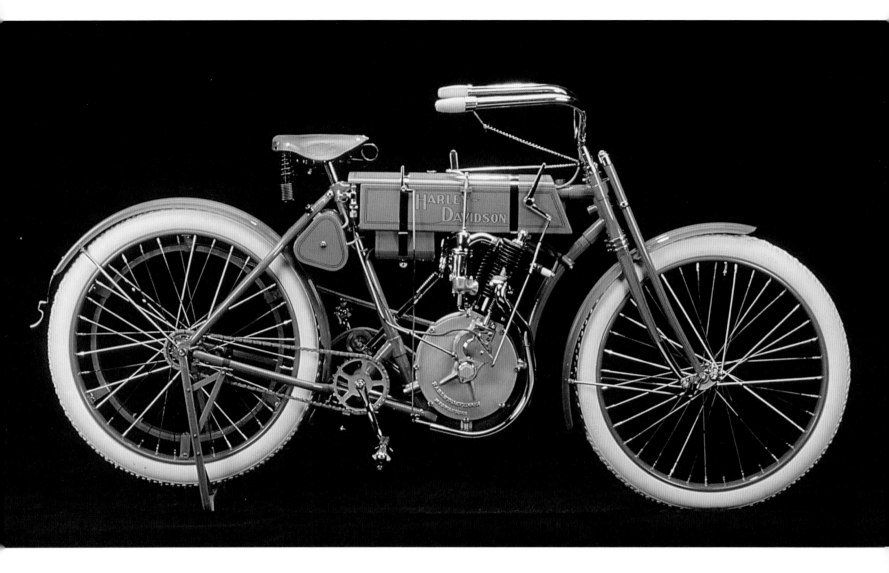

ABOVE: Production had increased to about 150 bikes by 1907. The Model 3 had minor improvements to make the engine more reliable.

RIGHT: Although visually there wasn't much to distinguish the 1907 from previous models, Harley engineers were also working on a V-twin engine that same year.

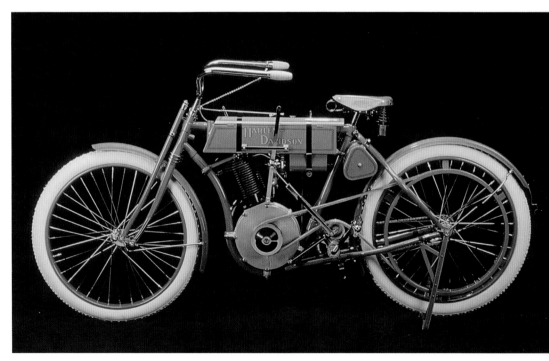

Working on the project with Arthur Davidson and another buddy named Henry Melk, who owned a lathe, Bill Harley tinkered through 1902 and into 1903, when Art's brother Walter came home expecting a ride.

The motor-bicycle wasn't finished, so Walter joined in. Less of a dreamer perhaps, Walter pushed aside old man Davidson's stuff in the backyard shed, and in the summer of 1903 they rolled out their proud creation. The motor-bicycle ran, but its motor wasn't powerful enough for Milwaukee's modest hills.

Here's where myth and confusion blurs the picture. A company document from 1907 clearly states that the machine finished in the "summer of 1903" was NOT the large, loop-frame bike we recognize today as the original Harley-Davidson, but a more primitive vehicle with a smaller engine attached to a pedal bicycle frame. No photograph of this first machine has ever surfaced. Confusing it with the second, and more advanced, loop-frame model was a natural trap for the unwary and careless, or those who later wanted to score points for advertising purposes. That's what happened.

But don't consider the 1901–1903 motor-bicycle a failure or an object of derision. Our heroes learned fast. First, they needed a bigger motor. They may have found it in the machine shop of Arthur's pal and another Milwaukee legend, famed outboard motor builder Ole Evinrude.

Evidence suggests that Bill Harley adapted Ole's single-cylinder engine for motorcycle service. Striking similarities exist between the Evinrude and Harley engines. This second engine had a 24.74-cubic-inch (405cc) displacement, considerably larger than the previous bicycle motor.

Things were moving fast in the local motorcycle industry. Both the Merkel Co. (Milwaukee) and Mitchell Co. (Racine) started building bicycle-like motorcycles in early 1901. In late 1902 (for the 1903 model year), both firms introduced totally new designs

ABOVE: This rare view shows the inside of Harley-Davidson's yellow brick factory around 1909–'10. In the early teens this almost new facility was razed and a much larger red brick factory was built on the same site. Engine Department foreman Max Kobs is seen at right.

ABOVE: By 1907 the Harley-Davidson was increasingly known for its excellent design, durability, and speed. From this date, factory output would double each year until Milwaukee would surpass industry leader Indian after World War I.

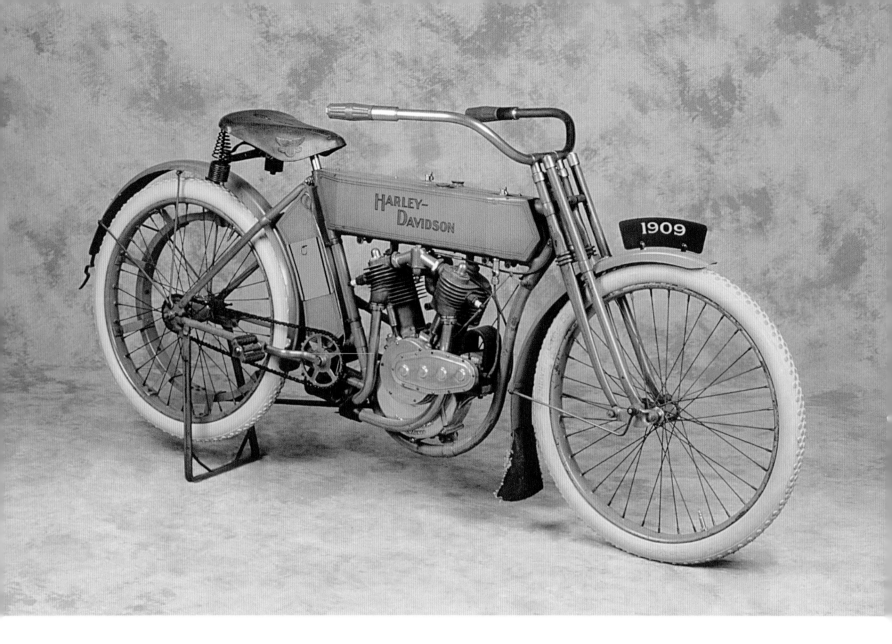

ABOVE: Less than thirty Model D bikes, sporting Harley's first V-twin engine, were made in 1909. Colors included Renault Grey, as seen here, and Black.

RIGHT: By 1912, Harley-Davidson motorcycles were being shipped to enthusiasts all around the world. Here a crated machine on the factory loading dock is destined for the country of Turkey.

based upon loop (Merkel) or cradle (Mitchell) frames. By abandoning the diamond-style bicycle layout, both the Merkel and Mitchell companies demonstrated a modern understanding of motorcycle engineering.

Thus, in the latter half of 1903, Bill Harley and the Davidson brothers had two innovative motorcycles built in the neighborhood to guide them. In fact, Harley's second design took strong cues from the Merkel, using a nearly identical extension fork and a very similar frame with a front downtube flowing around the engine in a continuous loop. As a result, the original Harley-Davidson came into existence using correct engineering principles with strong potential for future development.

One photo of this first "real" Harley-Davidson is known. It resembles, but is not identical to, the oldest bike in the H-D museum collection today.

The first prototype of this second H-D model, according to the previously quoted 1907 company source, was finished the "next season." Although it was begun in 1903, this would technically make it a 1904 model. At the time, however, no one was thinking about labels or model years. The 1904 finish date is almost certainly the reason Harley-Davidson made the 1954 bikes the 50th Anniversary models, rather than the 1953 bikes, as one might have expected. In 1978, when AMF/Harley-Davidson began celebrating anniversaries again, the distinction between the 1903 power-bicycle and the 1904 loop-frame prototype—apparently still recognized in 1954—had been lost.

Early histories and advertising literature handed out by the factory in the 1908–1916 period further cloud the picture, by providing a confusing hash of contradictory origin dates, incorrect model identification, and false claims. To be fair, accurate history was not Harley-Davidson's goal; selling motorcycles in a highly competitive market was.

ABOVE: The 1909 Model 5D represented Harley's venture into the V-twin market. The 45-degree V-twin engine developed approximately 7 horsepower.

BELOW: A large, easy-to-reach hand lever on the left side operated the freewheeling clutch assembly on the 1911 Model 6, making it easier to manage at low speeds.

After completing the second model sometime in 1904, our heroes' hobby took an entrepreneurial turn when a pal named Henry Meyer offered to buy that first machine.

Around that same time, a Chicago motorcycle buff named Carl H. Lang saw the Harley-Davidson. Lang liked the "Harley" so much (or "Davidson" as it was sometimes known) that he offered to sell the motorcycle in Chicago. In 1905 Harley and the Davidsons produced at least five motorcycles, three of which Lang took. In 1906 Lang took 24 of the 50 the group made. In 1907 he sold 84 out of 250.

In late 1906 Harley and the Davidsons built a small factory on Juneau Avenue (then Chestnut Street). In 1907, older brother Bill Davidson left the railroad to run the machine shop, instilling some locomotive durability into the two-wheeler. That September the founders formally incorporated as a business under the name Harley-Davidson Motor Co. Its mission statement: "Manufacture and sell motorcycles, motors, marine engines, and fixtures, and appliances."

BUILT ON HONOR

Up to that time, Harley-Davidson was largely a Milwaukee-Chicago phenomenon with a few machines sold in Philadelphia, Detroit, Minnesota, and even California. Perry Mack, Ralph Sporleder, and Walter Davidson had entered some midwestern races and won a few trophies, but they were small fish in a pond increasingly dominated by Indian—the winner of just about every important race in sight.

In 1910, Peter Olson of Cambridge, Wisconsin, bought this new battery ignition Harley single. Olson was one of Harley-Davidson's earliest customers when in 1905 this rural mail carrier bought one of the first Harleys ever produced.

In mid-1908 H-D's fame took off when Walter won the National Endurance Contest through New York State's Catskill Mountains. Sixty-five riders on seventeen different makes of motorcycle, including foreign bikes and the increasingly famous Indian, were entered. Just to show how regional Harley-Davidson was at this early date, the *New York Times* dubbed it the "Howard-Davidson."

Walter finished the contest with a perfect score of 1,000, but so did some others. What was outstanding about Walter's performance was his total time deviation of just eight minutes during the two-day, 356-mile course.

While many other machines had broken rims, cracked frames, or seized engines, Walter's bike came through without mishap. The top Indian riders had "Big Chief" Hendee and "Medicine Man" Hedstrom following in a Stevens-Duryea automobile filled with repair parts, but Walter had no backup vehicle, nor any spare parts.

Three days later, Walter went on to win the F.A.M. Economy Contest, going 50 miles on one quart and one ounce of gasoline—even beating bikes of smaller displacement. The judges were impressed. They awarded Walter five additional points for consistency and overall excellence. This 1,000-plus-5 win was one of the highest honors granted in early motorcycle competition.

Back in Milwaukee, Walter brought home a new spirit for Harley-Davidson. The Motor Company soon heralded his Diamond Medal win in full-page advertisements. This was the beginning of Harley-Davidson's national fame and fanatically loyal following.

H-D sales literature for 1909 touted a "Built on Honor" superior construction theme. The nickname "Gray Fellow" first came into use at this time (the term "Silent" was added

ABOVE: History credits 1911 as the year that Harley offered its first reliable—and successful—V-twin, but it was the single-cylinder Silent Gray Fellow that continued to lead sales.

BELOW: More cooling fins appeared on the single-cylinder, 30-cubic-inch workhorse engine for 1911.

ABOVE: A magneto ignition and rear-wheel clutch on the Model X8A highlighted some of the improvements for 1911.

BELOW: The rear-wheel clutch, as seen here on a 1912 Model 8, represents some of the technological innovations Harley-Davidson engineering created.

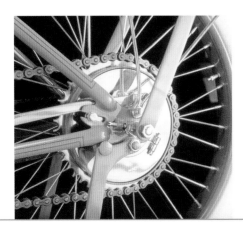

later). With a trusty Harley-Davidson, the advertisements announced, a person could ramble at will, exploring the countryside, and safely return home. From moonlit hilltops, one could marvel at America's romantic vastness, knowing it was attainable under the spinning wheels of the Harley-Davidson motorcycle.

Harley's advanced design, robust construction, and good-sized motor pushed Milwaukee ahead at a critical stage when a large percentage of motorcycle riders wanted rugged, economical transportation.

V-TWIN MANIA

The motorcycle was growing up fast. Riders' needs and desires were changing. Some were hitching up sidecars. Others wanted more hill-climbing oomph. Everyone wanted more mile-eating speed. These things were most easily obtained by adding a second cylinder. Glenn Curtiss had done it in 1903 with America's first production V-twin. And although Harley-Davidson had a V-twin prototype finished by late 1906, and advertised V-twins in 1907, 1908, 1909, and 1910, only a handful were produced during that period. Harley was tardy to adopt the V-twin design because demand for the single was so strong that a twin seemed unnecessary. Besides, technical difficulties with the suction intake valves used on all pre-1911 H-D twins tarnished Harley's sterling reputation for reliability.

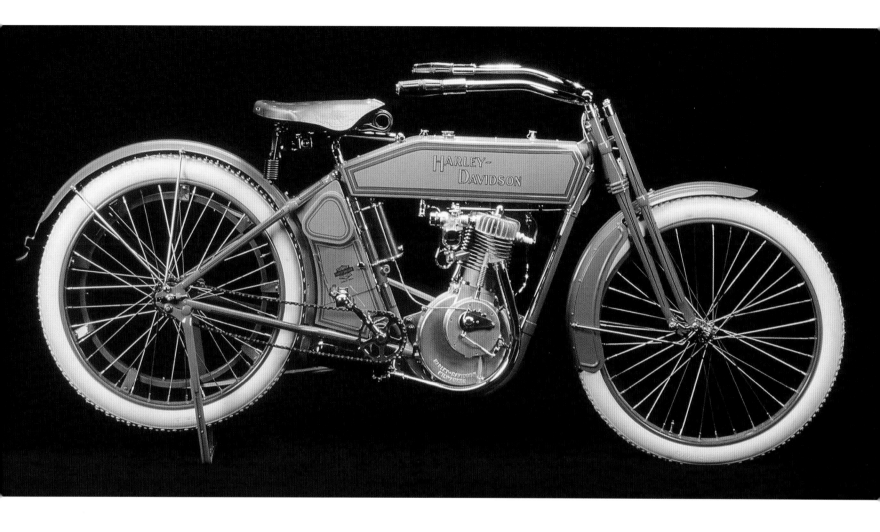

ABOVE: The evolutionary process continued for 1912. The new X8 shown here illustrates the rear bend in the frame rails that lowered seat height compared to previous models.

LEFT: Components for every motorcycle were carefully crafted and assembled by hand to assure durability and high quality. This scene is a glimpse inside H-D's tank shop around 1915.

ABOVE: H-D factory salesman George Puls hits the road with a two-speed twin in 1914. Harley-Davidson's founders liked its employees to use the firm's product for transportation purposes whenever they could, thereby demonstrating their confidence in Harley-Davidson reliability.

LEFT: Harley's first multispeed transmission appeared in 1914 with the Model C's two-speed configuration.

FROM MOONLIT HILLTOPS, ONE COULD MARVEL AT AMERICA'S ROMANTIC VASTNESS, KNOWING IT WAS ATTAINABLE UNDER THE SPINNING WHEELS OF A HARLEY-DAVIDSON MOTORCYCLE.

ABOVE: Motorcycle girls and Harley-Davidson employees Crystal Haydel and Lillian Hauerwas take this single-cylinder machine down a country road around 1911. Crystal worked at Harley-Davidson as assistant to president Walter Davidson and served as de facto office manager.

BELOW: If two speeds are good, then three speeds must be better, which resulted in the 1915 Model F's new three-speed transmission.

Once Harley perfected mechanical intake valves in 1911, the twin quickly overtook the single, and by 1913 the majority of Harley-Davidsons sold were V-twins. The bigger and heavier V-twin brought forth new challenges. Riders started their bikes by peddling or pushing and then jumping on, but the heavier V-twin made this run-and-jump-on business difficult. As one angry rider said, "To run along and then throw oneself on is good enough for young boys to do, but for a person over forty-five or fifty, it is a dangerous practice."

In 1907, Harley-Davidson became the first American motorcycle to offer a clutch as an option. In 1908, Harley offered an optional Lang two-speed transmission. Neither caught on. The vast majority of Harleys rolled out as single-speeds, using a simple belt-tensioning device. By 1912, as the bikes got bigger and heavier, Harley came back with a better clutch. With a clutch, riders could start from a standstill, without any foot or pedal assistance. At a stop, one could disconnect the engine from the drive.

Steep hills, city traffic, and sidecars stimulated the multispeed transmission. In 1914, H-D offered a rear-hub two-speed, and in 1915 the company introduced a modern enclosed three-speed running in oil. That same year electric lighting appeared, and in 1916 the kick-starter was first used. With these features, the modern Harley-Davidson platform was established. Except for electric start and foot shift, the basic design has not changed significantly to this day.

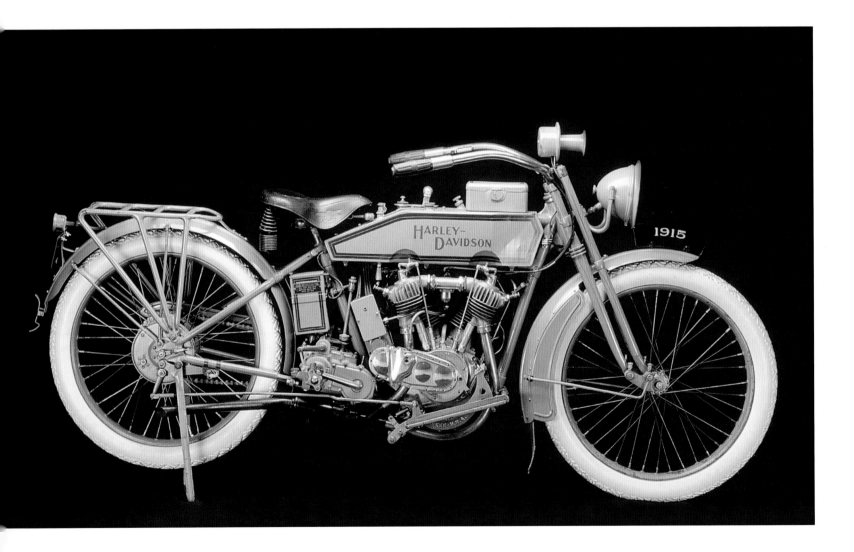

ABOVE: The three-speed transmission proved especially popular for customers, as represented by sales—the Model F outsold all other Harley models combined for 1915.

LEFT: Sidecars were popular items from 1910 to 1920. This 1916 Model J also had a three-speed transmission and electrical system for its lights, generator, and horn.

RIGHT: Affordability has always been a factor in Harley's marketing, and in 1915, the Model E represented the Motor Company's lowest-priced V-twin.

BELOW: By 1916, styling included valanced front fenders, a storage rack over the rear fender, and footboards for the rider's feet.

The early teens were a golden era for Harley-Davidson. America was prosperous, the motorcycle market was expanding, and Milwaukee was exporting Silent Gray Fellows around the world. Milwaukee riders were having fun putting on Goodfellowship Tours. These set the pattern for the gypsy tours and rallies of later decades. With a sidecar, the motorcycle could still compete with the automobile's family-carrying capacity. All this helped Harley-Davidson grow from 1,149 bikes built in 1909 to 16,924 in 1916.

That latter year, the original 1904 Harley-Davidson prototype is noted for the last time. In 1912–1913, it had been promoted in advertisements as having accumulated "100,000 miles" under a series of owners, beginning with Henry Meyer and ending with Stephen Sparough. In 1916, it was on display in C. H. Lang's Chicago dealership. Then it disappears from the historical record. For you get-rich-quick types, the original Harley is still out there, somewhere, waiting to be rediscovered.

THE GRAY FELLOW TURNS GREEN

In 1917 America entered World War I. For the first time, Harley-Davidson was drawn away from the consumer marketplace to dabble with motorcycles for war purposes. Bill Harley mounted machine guns on special sidecar rigs that first chased Pancho Villa along the Mexican border and later saw service when America entered World War I.

Sidecars came in a variety of configurations. This 1917 Model 17C carries a wicker-chair design on its right side.

A new standard color greeted Harley customers for 1917. Olive Green replaced the familiar gray as the base color for all models.

Harley-Davidson did not actively pursue big military contracts, but catered to US riders. Dealers could get new bikes and replacement parts until the last six months of the war in 1918, when the US Army took about 8,000 H-D motorcycles.

During the war Harley-Davidson's reliability was again demonstrated. As the late William H. Davidson once told me, "Harley got its deepest breath over in the mud in France."

In 1917 Harley-Davidson switched color from the traditional gray to military olive drab. Since I've never seen a reason given for this critical change, I'll offer one. Because Milwaukee was heavily ethnic German, that city had been slow to jump on the patriotic bandwagon. So slow, in fact, that as American isolationist sentiment changed to support of England and France, some had branded Milwaukee subversive. In the Harley family, there's a legend of government agents watching the house because Bill Harley had married Anna Jachthuber, whose parents were from Germany.

After 1908, the Harley-Davidson had worn gray paint (before that it was usually black), and the Silent Gray Fellow nickname was world famous. But as patriotic sentiment grew heated against all things German (sauerkraut became liberty cabbage and Milwaukee's Germania statue was sold for scrap), one might speculate that "Gray Fellow" was too close for comfort to the fellows wearing field-gray uniforms in Kaiser Bill's army.

LEFT: Early efforts to turn Harleys into fighting motorcycles were hampered by deep mud and other difficulties of trench warfare. Here the front fenders on these military machines have been removed due to sticky clay-mud during field testing south of Milwaukee in 1916.

BELOW: V-twin models with multispeed transmissions were the top sellers for 1917. Three-speed models included the Model 17F and the Model 17J, which also had a full electrical system.

ABOVE: As if to celebrate the end of the World War I, this 1919 Model J boasts a lively color scheme and nickel-plated components.

RIGHT: Demand for motorcycles grew so quickly that the modest yellow brick factory of 1908–1909 was soon dwarfed by a massive, five-story red brick addition built starting in 1910. Several more large additions would soon follow.

And doesn't the word *silent* imply stealth, secrecy, and eavesdropping? These were not desirable attributes in a country suddenly obsessed with enemy agents and espionage, where attacks against citizens suspected of mixed loyalty were common. Goodbye silent gray, hello army green.

BEST IN THE WORLD

By 1920, Harley-Davidson seemed on top of the world. Milwaukee built what was widely acknowledged as the best heavyweight motorcycle available anywhere. Milwaukee's dealership network was the envy of the industry. Company advertising was lavish, often artistically beautiful. The company had been solvent and profitable in every year of existence. The factory had grown from a 10x15-foot woodshed in 1903 to a massive six-story red brick complex stretching along Chestnut Street and around the corner on 37th (now 38th) Street, encompassing a total of 600,000 square feet of floor space.

Because of the demand for more powerful and faster motorcycles, Harley-Davidson came out with a 74-cubic-inch Big Twin in 1921. Some, however, were calling for even bigger motors displacing 80 or 100 cubic inches.

But there was reason to worry. American motorcycle registrations had peaked in 1920, after which a decline of 10,000–15,000 per year set in. In 1921, an economic recession caused Harley-Davidson to show a loss for the first time. Another sales drop in 1924 caused the Motor Company to post another loss. During these years people were switching from motorcycles to four-wheeled transportation. The trend was so serious that Harley-Davidson's founders gloomily predicted, "The pleasure sport riding

BECAUSE MILWAUKEE WAS HEAVILY ETHNIC GERMAN, THAT CITY HAD BEEN SLOW TO JUMP ON THE PATRIOTIC BANDWAGON.

The Model WF's engine was placed low in the frame. The 36-cubic-inch engine developed about 6 horsepower.

Pretty California girls in swimsuits became part of the Harley-Davidson advertising world beginning around 1923.

IN 1925, THE COMPANY HAD TAKEN OUT A PATENT ON A SHAFT-DRIVE SYSTEM. THE 1928 REPORT IS PROOF IT CONSIDERED PUTTING IT ON A PRODUCTION BIKE.

motorcycle is largely a thing of the past in this country and not to be depended upon for future business."

While some expected the faithful to come back, few would. The founders believed that the future lay in police sales and commercial delivery motorcycles, plus strong foreign demand. Such a policy would have doomed Harley-Davidson in time. The company needed an entirely new strategy for the American rider. But this would take time and agony to figure out.

In the early 1920s, overseas markets that buoyed up stagnant domestic growth were critical for H-D. Having shown its worth in World War I, the Harley-Davidson had largely pushed aside inferior British twins in overseas markets.

The Brits, however, came back strong with a new approach. In the early 1920s, they began building innovative models with more speed in a smaller package, bikes using advanced overhead-valve, single-cylinder technology. In 1924, readers of *MotorCycling* were stunned by a report of the 350cc overhead-camshaft Chater-Lea-Blackburne breaking the 100-mile-per-hour speed barrier at 6,000 rpm. This was amazing news in a nation where big, low-revving V-twins were the standard. It intrigued the founders, who were trying to fathom a changing marketplace. In 1926, Walter Davidson said, "Way back in 1905, |190|6, |190|7, |190|8 . . . the single-cylinder motorcycle was used partly as a sporting proposition and also very largely as economical transportation. The automobile was high-priced; the cheapest car in the neighborhood of $1,000, whereas your motorcycle sold in the

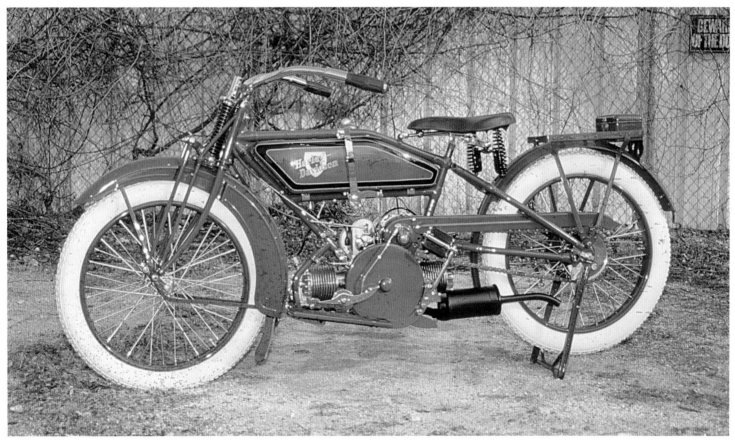

TOP: Among Harley's most unusual designs ever was the 1919 Model WF that was powered by a horizontally opposed twin-cylinder engine displacing 36 cubic inches.

BOTTOM: The white tires on this 1919 Model WF are indicative of what was offered for motorcyclists during the 1910s and 1920s.

ABOVE: Early Harley gas tanks were works of art. Note the notches on the bottom for the valve pushrod mechanisms and the assortment of caps and a gauge up top.

BELOW: Harley's Model J was the most expensive model in the 1920 lineup, and it proved to be the best-selling model that year too.

neighborhood of $200." But times had changed. Milwaukee's Big Twin was now more expensive than Ford's cheapest car!

Since the single-cylinder motorcycle had largely gone out of existence, the motorcycle was now a Big Twin proposition. The days when youngsters learned to ride on a small bike and then moved up to a larger one were gone. With older riders switching to automobiles, domestic motorcycle sales were eroding at both ends.

THE SINGLE STAGES A COMEBACK

That situation inspired H-D to build a new single-cylinder model in the mid-1920s. It wasn't a decision arrived at easily, as earlier attempt to market bicycles (1918–1924) and the 35-cubic-inch (584cc) flat-twin Sport Model (1919–1923) had not been successful. This time the nudge came from Harley-Davidson's foreign dealers, who begged for a smaller motorcycle to compete with the increasingly successful European singles.

After evaluating foreign markets, the founders decided to fill the gap with a totally new 21-cubic-inch (350cc) machine built along the lines of the Big Twin. Study showed a motor of that size with a three-speed gearbox was the best combination. Harley-Davidson introduced the new Single for 1926 in both economical side-valve form that got 70–80 miles per gallon and 50–55 miles per hour, and in sporting overhead-valve form that could top 65.

Harley-Davidson bet big on this new small machine, taking out ads in general circulation magazines. But Harley's strategy to reintroduce the single-cylinder motorcycle to America was not successful. The American public didn't want a motorcycle for basic transportation. It had fallen in love with the automobile, and it wasn't coming back. Overseas, where it might have succeeded, murderous new tariffs in the "Sterling Bloc" soon knocked Milwaukee out of the running.

Disappointment with the Single sent Harley-Davidson reeling back to the other extreme of the market—bigger engines and more cylinders. But while the Single was unsuccessful in the Sales Department, it would play an unexpected and unique role in H-D's eventual breakthrough success.

A HIDDEN ROOM AT HARLEY-DAVIDSON

Harley test rider and factory racer Albert "Squibb" Henrich tells a story from the 1920s that involves a mystery in the 1911 portion of the Juneau Avenue factory. To date, the mystery has not been solved.

During lunch one day, Squibb and Edwin "Sherbie" Becker were talking about old bikes in the Testers' Room in the western end of the factory basement. Then Sherbie asked Squibb to come around the corner near the elevator. Pointing to a spot on the massive concrete walls, Sherbie told Squibb that old belt-drive motorcycles were walled up back in there.

BELOW: A 74-cubic-inch V-twin was offered for the first time in 1921, but even so, the Model J and its 60-cubic-inch engine was the top seller for the year.

Squibb was an honest guy. I believe he described the story as best he could remember. So what gives? Is the story myth or true?

Perhaps it's a bit of both.

Squibb believed "the big boys"—the founders—knew about this cache of early bikes walled up in the basement. But in considering it over the years, I don't think that could be right. If the founders had known, you'd expect their descendants would know too—the children and grandchildren of the original Harleys and Davidsons. But I've asked some of them, and none knew of this hidden room story.

After considering the possibilities, I believe that in 1911, when that portion of the factory was under construction, an order came down from the "big boys" to clean up the "old junk" in the existing shop next door. This was a time of major model changes at Harley-Davidson. Two years earlier, it had issued its first replacement parts catalog, covering the 1909 model, but nothing earlier. This suggests that in 1911, H-D considered everything on hand from 1908 back obsolete and not worth saving. Just possibly, that accounts for the old motorcycles or parts that Sherbie was talking about.

I've heard other firsthand accounts of vintage H-D stuff buried in Milwaukee area landfills or dumped into Lake Michigan, so it seems possible that instead of calling the junk man in 1911 to cart that early stuff away, some of the guys—including Sherbie—simply dumped it all into an open excavation of the new factory, where it was soon covered over or walled up. The hidden room may simply have been an easy way to dispose of old junk.

A series of minor improvements, such as increased engine cooling fins and more durable exhaust valves, breathed new life into the venerable 60-cubic-inch V-twin like this Model F.

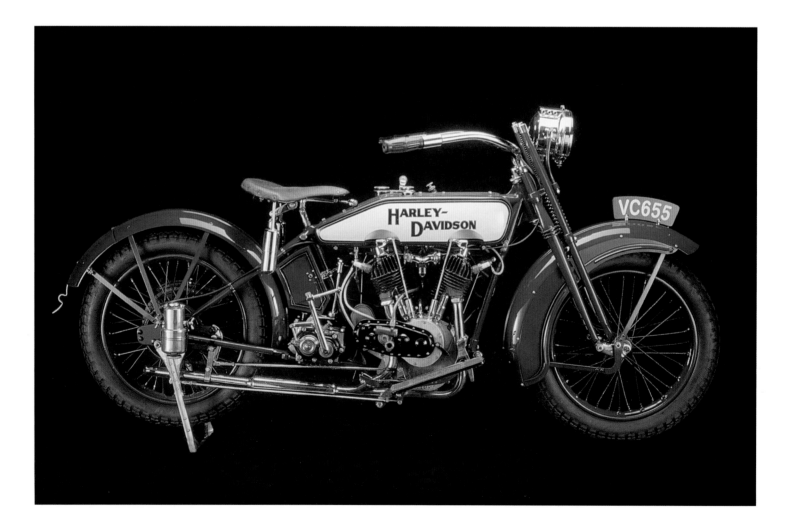

REGAINING GROUND

In early 1927, Arthur Davidson took four tanks enameled in maroon, light green, police blue, and light blue to the New York motorcycle show. H-D finally realized that riders wanted livelier colors than military drab.

While Harley was updating styling, it was also instilling new life into the dealer network and club scene. Both had stagnated after World War I. As Walter Davidson told dealers in 1926, "The day of selling motorcycles sitting in your store, waiting for the customer to come to you has gone by." Harley-Davidson tried to eliminate its more complacent and ossified agents. Milwaukee dealer Bill Knuth, who had worked at the Harley factory as early as 1911, founded the Cream City Motorcycle Club for Milwaukee riders. He put on activities like the Badger Derby, Midnight Mystery Tour, and Knuth's Kollege, which combined history, mechanical tips, riding lore, and good food—and brought many riders into the sport.

FOUR-CYLINDER SHAFT DRIVE EXPERIMENTAL

Harley's earlier prediction that the sporting motorcycle market was dying turned out to be wrong. More aggressive sales techniques and a revitalized club scene showed there was still great interest in motorcycling. Sales picked up and Harley-Davidson built nearly 24,000 motorcycles in 1929. Further factory expansion was considered. As Walter Davidson reported, "In the pleasure field there seems to be a very great market, and this can be greatly stimulated by bringing out new and better models."

ABOVE: The Model JE was the top seller for 1924. New fenders highlighted its styling.

BELOW: Reliability was one of the key selling features for the Model JE and other models for 1924. A dozen grease fittings made lubrication servicing easier for owners.

ABOVE: In 1925, a new, lower frame greeted customers. Harley advertising touted the Model JD frame as the new Stream-Line.

RIGHT: The sleek gas tank and upright battery are two of the standout styling features for 1925 Model JDs.

The new and better models that Walter had in mind would retire the old F-head V-twin still built to 1911 designs. The next generation of engines, introduced in 1929, would be side valves—a configuration Indian had done well with over the years.

But Harley had bigger plans. Much bigger. Late in 1928 the Engineering Department laid out an ambitious strategy in a surviving company document titled *Report of Meeting to Decide on Models for 1930.* The proposed model lineup was more imaginative than anything H-D had attempted yet. Six separate models were based upon the following engine types: 21 and 30.50 singles; 45 and 74 twins; and 80- and 90-cubic-inch fours.

The 1928 *Report* gives brief descriptions of the proposed four-cylinder models:

80 Cubic Inch Chain-Drive Model

90 Cubic Inch Shaft-Drive Model

No further construction details are noted beyond a brief mention that both models were to incorporate a new low frame and new tanks.

The four-cylinder motors went beyond anything Harley-Davidson had ever built. It is believed they resembled two compact 45s placed side by side in a single crankcase and perhaps with cylinders cast in pairs—almost like something you'd find in an air-cooled automobile engine. The frame for these V-4 models was probably not the single downtube VL type, but a new double downtube cradle frame similar to that used with the later 61 overhead-valve Knucklehead. The 90-inch shaft-drive model is the more fascinating of these V-4s. In 1925, the company had taken out a patent on a shaft-drive system. The 1928 *Report* is proof it considered putting it on a production bike. In 1929, William S. Harley recommended that a four-cylinder shaft-drive model be assembled and tested before deciding whether to produce it.

Sidecars remained somewhat popular through the 1920s. This 1925 Model JD attaches its sidecar to the right side.

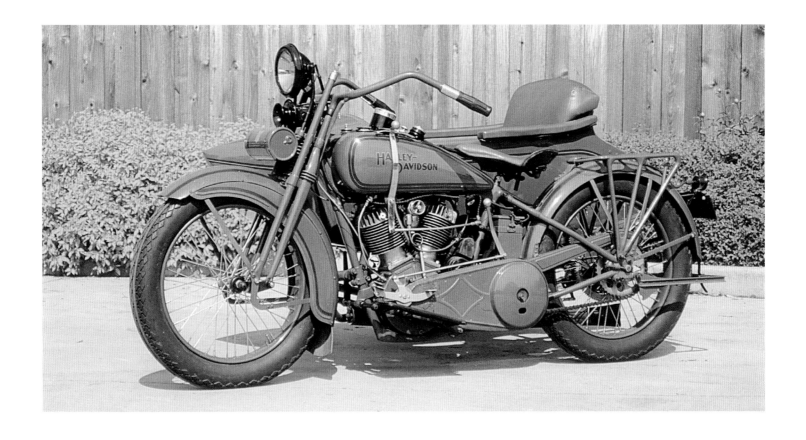

ABOVE: Speedometers were an option in 1925. This Model JD has its speedo mounted to the gas tank.

BELOW: Harley marketed the single passenger sidecar as the Model LT, selling for $100 in 1925. It even had a hinged door for the passenger!

Years ago, Squibb Henrich told another story about his factory test riding days, of taking out an experimental shaft-drive V-engine Harley. At that time he guessed it was a 45-inch V-twin, but now I'd bet anything the shaftie Henrich rode was the 90-inch V-4.

According to Henrich (who was remembering the event sixty years later), Harley built three prototype machines that were kept at a secret base in Reedsburg, with testing done up near Wildcat Mountain.

When asked what he thought of the shaftie, Heinrich replied, "Oh, I liked it. There wasn't nothing it couldn't do. It was a powerful machine, quiet, smooth, as smooth as a Henderson Four on takeoff. You didn't have to worry about sand or mud. You could ride axle deep and never wear it out like a chain. The shaft-drive worked beautifully with those rubber cushions to take up the torque."

To date, no factory photos of these V-4 Harleys have surfaced. And as we all know, neither the 80-inch chain or 90-inch shaft-drive V-4 were put into production. Yet if the machine was as good as old Squibby remembered, why wasn't it built? What happened?

The onset of the Great Depression may have been a contributing factor. But might other reasons have convinced H-D to cancel these stunning new models?

Perhaps. In 1929, the long-running lawsuit against Harley-Davidson by the Eclipse Company for infringement of a clutch patent came to a frightful conclusion. Harley-Davidson had been confident should it lose the case, at most $300,000 would be paid out. The judge, however, awarded a heart-stopping $1.1 million to Eclipse. In the final agreement, the founders had two weeks to fork over the money or lose the factory. Old timers say that Walter Davidson never got over the shock—the worst in the company's history—although harder times were yet to come.

While H-D had enough cash socked away in government securities to pay Eclipse off, it made the necessary high tooling costs of bringing out a completely new motorcycle platform an extravagance in light of the economic downturn, and the founders probably killed the V-4 project as a result.

Perhaps it was just as well. Harley-Davidson entered the 1930s with the uninspiring but cheap-to-build VL as the big bike in the model lineup, and even these would be a tough sell. A luxury V-4 would have had little chance of success in the dismal market environment of the Great Depression.

Thus ended the early years of Harley-Davidson. Starting as backyard dreamers, the founders established the fundamentals of a world-famous motorcycle company based on sound engineering, manufacturing, and marketing principles. During this period, Harley-Davidson gathered a fanatically loyal following that is still going strong 100 years later.

The JD was, by far, Harley's top-selling model for 1927. A new ignition system found its way into the design that year.

CHAPTER 2

THE FLATHEAD ERA

BY JERRY HATFIELD

THE SIDE-VALVE ENGINE, AN ARCHAIC DESIGN NOW CONFINED TO LAWN
MOWERS AND WEED WHACKERS, ONCE POWERED MANY OF THE WORLD'S HIGH-
PERFORMANCE MOTORCYCLES. THE SIDE-VALVE NAME COMES FROM
THE LOCATION OF THE VALVES IN A POCKET OFF TO THE SIDE OF THE
CYLINDER BORE. THE VALVES ARE UPSIDE-DOWN AND THE STEMS PARALLEL
TO THE BORE. THE UNDERSIDE OF THE CYLINDER HEAD CONSISTS OF A FLAT
SURFACE INTO WHICH A SLIGHT CAVITY IS FORMED TO ALLOW THE VALVES
TO OPEN AND THE COMBUSTION PROCESS TO START. WERE IT NOT FOR THE
COOLING FINS, THE TOP OF THE HEADS WOULD ALSO BE FLAT, EARNING THIS
TYPE OF ENGINE THE NICKNAME "FLATHEAD."

the *new* improved Harley-Davidson *for* 1931

ABOVE: Second-generation family member, William H. Davidson, appeared in this 1931 Harley-Davidson ad. After finishing college he joined the company full-time in 1928. Upon the death of his uncle, company president Walter Davidson in 1942, William H. Davidson was made Motor Company president, a position he held until 1971.

RIGHT: The 1926 Model B was powered by a 21-cubic-inch, single-cylinder engine. Top speed was rated at 60 miles per hour.

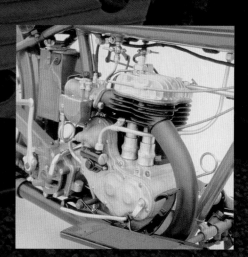

For a given capacity, flatheads burn more fuel than overhead-valve engines. For a given performance level, a flathead engine needed to be larger, and thus heavier, than a comparable overhead. On paper the flathead design is inferior to an overhead-valve configuration, but in the mid-1920s, inferior fuels narrowed the gap between flathead and overhead performance. Because of the poor quality of gasoline, overhead-valve engines were forced to use low-compression pistons, so flatheads weren't that much weaker than overheads until the arrival of tetraethyl lead at service stations in 1924. The availability of more efficient (and more expensive) fuel along with motorcyclists' rising expectations for performance doomed the flathead design to the scrap heap of history. For a time during the first half of the twentieth century, however, the flathead reigned supreme.

ABOVE: All new for 1926, the Model B represented Harley-Davidson's return to a single-cylinder engine design, although the Model J V-twins continued to be the top sellers.

FIRST OF THE HARLEY-DAVIDSON FLATHEADS

As 1920 drew near, Harley-Davidson had the largest motorcycle factory in the world, but H-D sales had leveled off. The heady years of explosive growth, in which the Harley-Davidson factory had annually doubled its output, were behind the company. To keep growing, Harley-Davidson needed to bring new people into motorcycling.

Harley-Davidson F-head (or inlet-over-exhaust, the combustion chamber design used on most early motorcycles) V-twins were all the things that sporting motorcyclists liked: big, noisy, rough, oily, and fast, which of course meant that the car crowd loathed them. To convert car people into motorcycle people, Harley's new model would be the opposite: shorter, lower, lighter, cleaner, smoother, and quieter. The new Harley would have enough muscle for all normal riding conditions, yet run quietly to avoid the suggestions of speed and danger.

Harley-Davidson introduced the missionary motorcycle designed to bring in new riders in 1919. Called the "Sport," the new model featured a 584cc (35.6-cubic-inch) engine, twice the size of the Indian light twin then on the market. The Harley sales catalog proclaimed "Not a lightweight!" This was the first flathead middleweight motorcycle built by one of the three major American companies—Harley-Davidson, Indian, and Excelsior. The Sport, the first American middleweight with an opposed cylinder configuration, featured other innovations for the American market, including unit construction of the engine and three-speed transmission, helical gear primary drive, and a wet clutch.

The Sport engine spun as smoothly as a turbine. The sweetly running middleweight seemed to have it all, and first-year Sport sales were brisk. But a year later, Indian brought

ABOVE: Harley-Davidson factory test riders Al Henrich and Clarence Held on the road in 1925. These guys put on hundreds of miles every day in the countryside surrounding Milwaukee. Bikes tested were both standard road models and secret experimental jobs.

RIGHT: For 1927, the single-cylinder models, such as this Model BA, were given a few improvements that included a new muffler, stronger frame and gas tank, and reinforced engine cases.

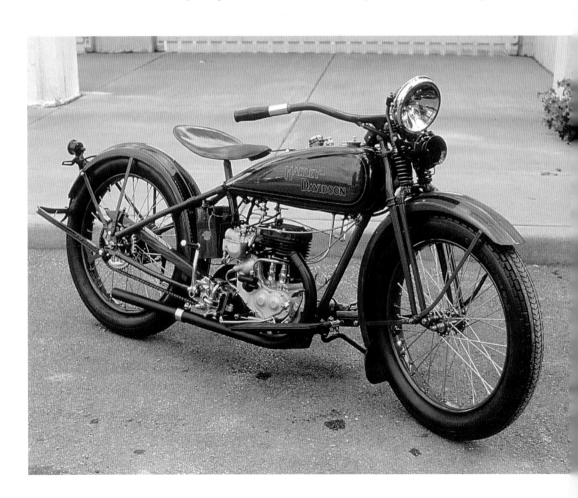

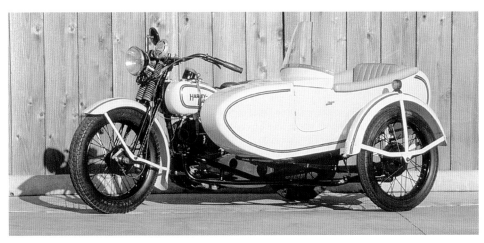

TOP: The new 74-cubic-inch engine offered more power, setting the stage for what was in store for coming years.

BOTTOM LEFT: By 1930, sidecars had become rather sophisticated in design. Harley even offered them in two-passenger configurations.

BOTTOM RIGHT: The venerable F-head design was dropped completely from the lineup in 1930, leaving two side-valve designs, the 45 and the 74, which is shown here.

ABOVE: Harley enthusiasts looking for more performance in 1931 reached for the Model VL. Its 74-cubic-inch engine boasted high-compression pistons.

RIGHT: The compact dimensions of the 45-cubic-inch, side-valve engine underscores the simplistic, yet classic, lines of the early flathead models.

out the 1920 600cc Scout V-twin, with the traditional "potato-potato-potato" V-twin sound. The peppier Scout out-sported the Sport, so survival of the Harley middleweight hinged on its missionary effectiveness.

Unfortunately, the Sport cost too much. Equipped with lights, the motorcycle sold for $445, roughly $9,000 in today's money. Used Model T Fords could be bought for less, so the Sport couldn't compete as basic transportation. At $485, the 1,000cc (61-cubic-inch) Harley-Davidson V-twin cost only 9 percent more than the 584cc Sport, so the middleweight couldn't compete with the bigger Harleys for the sporting business. Thus, the Sport was on the market only through 1923. Sport sales totaled 9,130 over five seasons. As 1923 drew to a close, the Sport missionary movement had failed, and Harley-Davidson again was an all F-head marquee.

LET'S TRY AGAIN

Somewhere in the Harley-Davidson dealer network, a rider bought the last Sport in late 1923. Six months later, the company decided to build another bike for commuters and penny pinchers. Why? For two reasons. First, management viewed the Sport's demise as the result of having produced an overengineered and overpriced motorcycle. The second reason for a new model was the strength of the foreign markets, particularly British Commonwealth nations, where the rugged Milwaukee brand was well suited to colonial rough roads. Harleys sold well south of the equator, in Africa, Australia, and New Zealand. These Southern Hemisphere markets had riding seasons the opposite of the United States, and supplying them enhanced Harley-Davidson production efficiency by leveling off peaks and valleys.

Worldwide, the most popular motorcycles were chain-driven 250cc or 350cc flathead single-cylinders with three-speed hand-shifted transmissions, the kind of motorcycles

ABOVE: The one-year-only 1953 side-valve KK model combined racing camshafts, polished ports, and a ball-bearing crank fitted into a road model chassis for performance-oriented riders. Today an original condition KK is a rare collector's item.

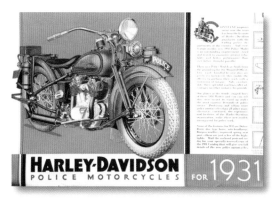

ABOVE: Well-equipped motorcycles for law enforcement purposes made up an important part of Harley-Davidson business during the Great Depression years when other buyers were far and few between.

LEFT: By the 1930s motorcycle fashion assumed a new direction with emphasis on club uniforms and a clean, respectable, para-military look. This is a rally at Elkhart Lake, Wisconsin, in 1940. The bike is 1938 45-inch model WL side-valve twin.

ABOVE: Small dealerships like this one in Manitowac, Wisconsin, were critical to Harley's survival in the economic downturn of the 1930s. In addition to the handful of new bikes they might have sold, shops like this also repaired and maintained any police or municipal motorcycles used in the area.

RIGHT: Tall boots, leather jackets, flying helmets, and goggles were standard motorcycle garb in the 1930s. Not only practical, this apparel looked good too. These riders are members of an Appleton, Wisconsin, motorcycle club in the 1930s.

that Harley-Davidson could build at rock-bottom prices. The one-lungers came out in late 1925 as 1926 models. Because cost containment was critical, a variation of the single was offered with magneto ignition but no lights. The stateside price of this minimal motorcycle was just $210, about half that of the no-frills Sport once offered.

For 1930, the factory brought out a 500cc (30.5-cubic-inch) flathead single. The 350cc singles were offered for the seasons of 1926 through 1930 in both flathead and overhead versions, and as flatheads only from 1931 through 1934.

Harley-Davidson singles lasted nearly twice as long as the Sport, and singles sales were about triple that of the Sport, but by 1933, at the bottom of the Great Depression, production and sales of all Harley-Davidsons were down to about 10 percent of plant capacity. Sales of the singles were hardest hit, falling to just over 300. This seems odd on first thought, since a low-bucks bike would seem to have been just the ticket for Depression-era buyers, but two factors contributed to low sales of the single. First, newly raised Commonwealth tariffs killed Southern Hemisphere sales overnight. Second, Harley's lightweights competed with their larger models. Customers who could barely afford new singles were just as likely to buy used Forty-Fives or Seventy-Fours for about the same price. Besides, if you rode a single amid the twin-cylinder crowd, you were considered what today we would call a "nerd." The factory justified continued singles offerings by assembling bikes from stocks of leftover parts.

More than 27,000 singles were sold during the nine seasons of 1926 through 1934, the great bulk of them flatheads. Though singles sales finally dived, one of every four Harley-Davidsons sold during the era was a single. The one-lungers had earned their keep, but it was time to move on with an all twin-cylinder lineup.

ABOVE: New paint graphics, as seen on this Model D, were found on the 1931 models.

BELOW: By the 1930s, motorcycle designs were becoming more intricate in their execution. The amp gauge on this 1931 Model D helped keep the rider informed about the electrical charge.

ABOVE: Hal Decker's VL is up to its hubs in mud near Lyndon Station, Wisconsin, in 1935. Earlier generations of Harley riders used their Big Twins like today's high-tech adventure bikes, while modern Harleys have become a road-only proposition.

LEFT: Accessories have always been a major component to the Harley marketing equation, and this 1932 Model V boasts a few interesting add-ons.

CUSTOMERS WHO COULD BARELY AFFORD NEW SINGLES WERE JUST AS LIKELY TO BUY USED FORTY-FIVES OR SEVENTY-FOURS FOR ABOUT THE SAME PRICE.

ABOVE: Even though the Great Depression stifled the American economy in 1933, Harley's two leading models in sales were its most expensive models—the VL, shown here, and the VLD.

RIGHT: The promise of open road adventure attracted day-dreaming city workers as shown in this 1932 ad. The in-the-elements freedom of the motorcycle has always been one of its main attractions.

PLAN *NOW for a*
MOTORCYCLE
VACATION

RIDE to Vacationland this summer. Let older folks have the crowding cars and stuffy trains.

The Open Road for you—with a swift, powerful Harley-Davidson Motorcycle to zip you over roads and trails, free as the birds.

Of all happy, healthy outings there is none that can equal a Motorcycle Vacation. And it costs so little. Plan yours now—great riding weather is just around the corner . . . . . . Step into your nearest Harley-Davidson Dealer's. Look over the 1932 models. *Ask about his Pay-As-You-Ride Plan.*

Prices as low as $195

That's right—$195 at-the-factory buys a completely equipped motorcycle—the wonderful Harley-Davidson Single, speedy, powerful, economical.

Mail the Coupon for literature showing our full line of motorcycles and sidecars.

Ride a
HARLEY-DAVIDSON

HARLEY-DAVIDSON MOTOR COMPANY
Dept. P., Milwaukee, Wis.

Interested in your motorcycles.
Send literature.

Name

Address

My age is ☐ 16-19 years, ☐ 20-30 years, ☐ 31 years and up, ☐ under 16 years.
Check your age group.

THE BIG MOVE

The Harley-Davidson F-heads had put the Milwaukee brand on top in both the showrooms and on the racetrack. But the F-head V-twins were near the end of their development trail. Harley-Davidson began to consider replacing the F-head V-twins with either flathead or overhead-valve V-twins. Several F-head shortcomings motivated a change The inlet rockers were exposed to benefit from cooling air, which meant that oil mist settled over the engine and collected dust to produce grime. The exposed rockers promoted rapid wear, because dust mixed with oil seepage to produce a lapping compound. Consequently, F-heads required frequent rocker arm maintenance to keep in top tune. The exposed inlets pushrods and rocker arms also produced a clattering that didn't inspire confidence.

Harley-Davidson understood that overhead-valve engines were ultimately going to dominate the car and motorcycle markets. The question was when. Metallurgy in 1925 wasn't what it is today. Exhaust valves were particularly troublesome on air-cooled engines, which is why the Harley F-heads had two exposed rockers and valve stems and why overhead-valve motorcycles had four of these sets. For Harley, the appeal of high-performance overhead-valve engines was offset by the prospect of doubling the F-head grime, wear, and noise. Harley-Davidson was impressed by its great rival, Indian. The Indian flatheads had all the moving parts enclosed, side-stepping the F-head problems of wear, noise, and filth. In the street-racing wars, the Indian flatheads held their own. In the end, Harley opted for a near-term sure thing. Its next generation of V-twin motorcycles would be powered by flatheads.

ABOVE: The Model VLD had high-compression pistons, and it was affordable. The combination made it Harley's top-selling model in 1934.

A FALSE START

Harley-Davidson decided to launch the new flathead V-twin concept by entering the middleweight field, which the company had abandoned with the defunct Sport. Its reasoning was simple. At the time, prospective Harley buyers surveyed the dealers' floors and chose between a 270-pound 350cc single for $235 or a 500-pound 1,000cc V-twin for $335. Harley designed a 600cc (37-cubic-inch) flathead V-twin to plug the gap between these two machines and to compete head on with the same-sized flathead Indian Scout. Each 300cc cylinder of the proposed V-twin would generate less stress than the 350cc cylinder of the lightweight single, so many of the lightweight single parts could be used on the middleweight twin, resulting in substantial cost savings. But as Harley proceeded with planning on the 600cc V-twin, Excelsior introduced the F-head 750cc Super X V-twin, and then Indian launched its flathead 750cc Scout 45 V-twin. The appearance of these 750cc rivals forced Harley-Davidson to increase the size of the proposed middleweight to 750cc, and this delayed the debut of the model by a year or more.

ABOVE: Curvaceous fenders highlight the V-twin models of 1934. This profile of the VLD clearly shows the fenders' classic beauty.

LEFT: Harley-Davidson dealer Ray Tursky with female members of the Madison Motorcycle Club, 1937.

BELOW: The 1934 VLD motor was nicknamed the TNT Motor, based primarily on its high compression. Equally stunning was the two-tone paint job, seen here.

ABOVE: Newly completed Harley factory about 1915. Faded lettering can still be seen on the side of the building today.

RIGHT: Harley-Davidson Engineering Department, circa 1923–1924; William S. Harley (right).

THE FORTY-FIVE

The new Harley-Davidson Forty-Five 750cc flathead V-twin, introduced in 1929, was a handsome motorcycle. Part of the credit for the good looks went to the frame, which featured a straight front downtube. The straight front downtube left no room to mount a generator in front of the engine, so to accommodate the generator, the factory mounted the unit to the side of the engine. The factory aligned the generator with the front downtube to keep the lines smooth and flowing.

ABOVE: Records show that 4,527 customers stepped up to buy a Model VLD in 1934. The crisp lines and two-tone paint job on this VLD help explain why it was so popular.

LEFT: The Jack Pine Enduro in Lower Michigan was a 500-mile, two-day grind through deep sand, swamps, and red clay mud. First place winner in 1934 was Ray Tursky (center) on a 34VLD Big Twin, shown with fellow Fond du Lac, Wisconsin, club members Harvey Haase (left) and Adam Beyer (right).

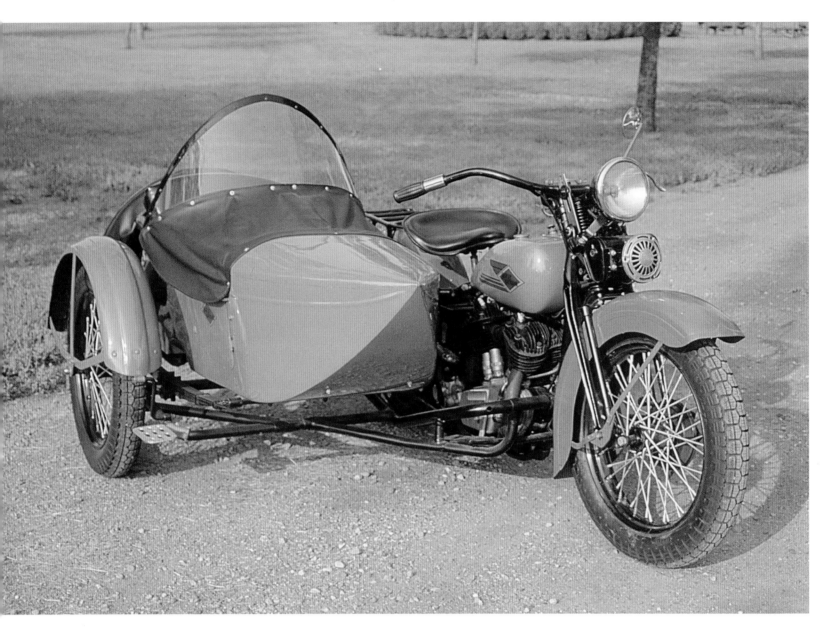

ABOVE: Sidecars continued their popularity into the 1930s. This rig is attached to a 1934 VLD.

RIGHT: Motorcycle parking at a rally in Wisconsin, 1930s.

The abundance of parts from the single-cylinder range emphasized the lightness of the Forty-Five and suggested good acceleration and responsive handling. With so much of the weight carried low to the ground, the Forty-Five seemed hardly heavier than the flathead single. However, as the fleet of new Forty-Fives fathered mileage, the use of so many singles' parts proved unwise. The clutch wasn't strong enough, and the engine was so low in the frame that the crankcase bottomed out during turns. Harley halted Forty-Five production in the spring of 1929 to correct these problems. Production of the revamped Forty-Fives continued through the 1931 season.

THE FLATHEAD BIG TWINS

For the 1930 season, Harley-Davidson replaced the last of the F-head engines with a 1,200cc (74-cubic-inch) flathead design. The new Model V, or Seventy-Four, as it came to be known, was pulled from the market shortly after its introduction in late 1929 because of technical problems, as had been the Forty-Five flathead before it. The flywheels proved

ABOVE: There were no quick-detach saddlebags in 1935. This Model VLD retains the leather-shrouded anchor points on the rear fender as evidence it can carry saddlebags.

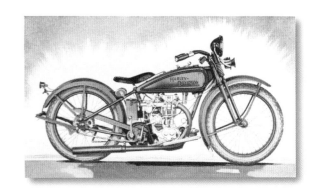

ABOVE: This profile of a 1935 VL shows how important styling was then, as it is now. The fenders were long and swooping, and the taillight emphasized the art deco styling of the era.

ABOVE: This 1930s-era Harley and sidecar have seen better days.

too light for American-style riding, and the lighter clutch springs proved too weak for American use. In early 1930, the factory shipped a modification kit to dealers, who rebuilt the Seventy-Fours. Dealers had to remove everything from the old frame, disassemble the engine, reassemble all engine parts to the new crankcase, remove and replace the clutch, then install everything into the new frame. And they did all this on their own dime, because the factory didn't compensate the dealers for the labor involved.

The new flathead Seventy-Fours produced about the same power as the last of the F-head V-twins, but since the V series weighed about 100 pounds more, acceleration was disappointing to sporting riders. The saving grace was considerably improved reliability. Dealers promoted long, fast club runs, during which the F-head Big Twins overheated and shed parts, while the new flathead Big Twins kept running and stayed together.

The reliable flathead V-twins arrived just as Americans fell in love with long-distance touring. Highways were being paved. Service stations blossomed, and they gave away detailed maps of the newly numbered national and state road systems. Aided by both the new road signs and maps, riders seldom got lost as in the F-head era. The new motel and fast-food industries were growing rapidly. Service stations emphasized clean restrooms, so riders and their dates didn't have to "pick flowers," the euphemism for relieving oneself behind the bushes. Along with better roads came faster speeds. Ever-smoother roads throughout the 1930s allowed faster speeds over longer stretches. The flathead V-twins met these new challenges far better than the old F-heads.

ABOVE: Even though the fabled overhead-valve E model had been introduced to the market the previous year, the UDH side-valve model was the company's second-best seller in 1937.

LEFT: High-compression pistons and a four-speed transmission made the UL and its 74-cubic-inch engine a favorite among customers in 1938.

RIGHT: The overhead-valve EL model debuted in 1936 and accounted for 1,526 units sold. This VLH was one of 2,046 sold the same year.

BELOW: The neutral position for the 1939 ULH's four-speed, hand-shift transmission was found between second and third gears—the only year it was offered as such.

The V series continued through 1936 with detail refinements. During this era, California dealer Tom Sifton was a styling pioneer. He fitted virtually all his new Harleys with custom-designed, high-rise, chrome-plated handlebars. The handlebars became part of the "California" look, which became increasingly popular on the West Coast. Harley-Davidson brought out the overhead-valve 1,000cc (61-cubic-inch) Knucklehead in 1936, but the company shrewdly continued to offer both flatheads and the Knuckleheads. For the 1937 season, Harley-Davidson outfitted the Seventy-Four and Forty-Five with recirculating (dry sump) oiling. These models were designated the U (Seventy-Four) and W (Forty-Five) series. An 80-cubic-inch flathead was offered as the Model VLH for 1935 and 1936, and as the Model UL for 1937 and 1940. By the 1941 season, Knuckleheads were outselling flathead Big Twins, so the Eighty was dropped to avoid competing with the new 1,200cc (74-cubic-inch) overhead-valve machines. After World War II, Knuckleheads dominated sales, and flathead Big Twins withered. The flathead Seventy-Four continued through the 1948 season, and the Forty-Five through the 1951 season.

FLATHEADS HELP WIN WORLD WAR II

The United States military used Harley-Davidsons for all its World War II needs. (Indians were limited to test programs and to use by Allied forces.) During the war, Harley-Davidson built more than 80,000 motorcycles for American and Allied forces. The great bulk of these were flathead Forty-Fives. Despite the photos and text in many magazine

ABOVE: Girl riders, 1930s.

BELOW: Harriet Mandy of Ladysmith, Wisconsin, with her own 1941 45-inch, side-valve model WL. Women riders go back to the earliest days of the sport but became more common in the 1930s–40s.

ABOVE: For many years, motorcycles played a key role in commerce as delivery vehicles. This 1938 Model U, including a spare tire, was set up as a package delivery model.

BELOW: Design genius William S. Harley (left) and Arthur Davidson with an XA sidecar machine early in World War II. The XA was based upon the German BMW horizontally opposed flat twin. This was one of the last photos ever taken of Mr. Harley, who died suddenly in 1943. He was active at his job as chief engineer until the final day of his life.

articles of the era, and Harley's proud advertisements, American and Allied forces didn't use motorcycles as combat vehicles. Instead, the army used them for military police activities, such as posting traffic directors along convoy routes. Harley-Davidson's continuous high wartime production rate kept the company running efficiently. Harley's war experience positioned the company for efficient motorcycle manufacturing when peace production returned in late 1945.

THE MODEL K: AN ANSWER TO THE BRITISH INVASION

In the late 1940s, many British bikes arrived on the American scene. Typically, these middleweight motorcycles featured telescopic forks, 500cc (30.50-cubic-inch) overhead-valve engines, hand-operated clutches, and four-speed foot-shifted transmissions. Many Brit-bike riders gave their motorcycles the California treatment, which included high-rise handlebars and cut-down or "bobbed" fenders. These imports weighed less than the Harley Forty-Fives and, coupled with more efficient engines and transmissions, performed better. Some imports even included rear suspensions. With the devaluation of British currency in 1949, the imports sold for about two-thirds the cost of Harley's Forty-Five. Harley's more costly Forty-Five, with its springer fork, rigid rear end, and three-speed, hand-shifted transmission, could not last against this competition.

To meet the challenge, Harley-Davidson brought out a new, technologically advanced middleweight, the Model K. The K featured a telescopic fork but upped the comfort ante by tossing in a long-travel swinging-arm rear suspension. The K layout was a trendsetter, and within a few years all rivals used a swinging-arm rear suspension. High-rise handlebars, the highest ever put on a stock Harley up to that time, conformed to

ABOVE: Kenosha, Wisconsin, Harley dealer Frank Ulicki (center) at a blindfold contest.

LEFT: An XA model during World War II.

THESE IMPORTS WEIGHED LESS THAN THE HARLEY FORTY-FIVES AND, COUPLED WITH MORE EFFICIENT ENGINES AND TRANSMISSIONS, PERFORMED BETTER.

RIGHT: Harley-Davidson supplied the US military with more than 90,000 WLAs for combat duty during World War II. This is a GI's eye-view of the venerable 45's controls.

BELOW: Adolph Roemer, Milwaukee Motorcycle Dispatch Corps, 1941–1942.

YOU DIDN'T SIT ON A K AT THE LOCAL HAMBURGER DRIVE-IN, YOU SAT IN THE K. THE MOTORCYCLE HAD A LOOK THAT WAS RIGHT FOR THE TIMES.

the California style. Harley-Davidson didn't build cut-down bikes in those days, so the K featured full fenders with the classic Milwaukee flair. Yet, the overall lines of the K mimicked the cut-down bobber look. Behind the long front fork and the high-rise bars was a high-rise fuel tank. But the tank swept dramatically down as it swept back, making the solo saddle seem lower than it was. You didn't sit *on* a K at the local hamburger drive-in, you sat *in* the K. The motorcycle had a look that was right for the times.

The model K featured a unit-construction engine and transmission that was stronger than the old separate engine and gearbox setup. The four-speed foot-shift transmission met the British opposition head on.

In contrast to these sophisticated features, the K continued with the side-valve engine configuration. The size of the 750cc K powerplant was supposed to compensate for its antiquated valvetrain design. Two facts diminished the comparative performance of the K. First, the Model K weighed 450 pounds, but typical British 500cc motorcycles weighed

TOP: Desperate times call for desperate measures, and so Harley-Davidson tried new and different designs for the war. The Model XS represented one of those designs.

BOTTOM LEFT: This Model XA has a utility box—perhaps to hold spare ammunition—attached to its leading-link fork.

BOTTOM CENTER: The XA engine was unique among American designs. Based on a captured German-built BMW, the engine has horizontally opposed cylinders.

BOTTOM RIGHT: Goodyear supplied the XA's balloon tires, and a pair of hydraulic shock absorbers helped smooth the ride up front.

about 350 pounds. Second, the K was targeted at the wrong competitors. The British 650cc (40-cubic-inch) overhead-valve entries from Triumph and BSA, which appeared as 1950 models, beat the Harley K to the market. With 30 percent more power than the K, and being hardly any heavier, the 650cc imports outpaced the Harley K.

THE KH CLOSES THE GAP

For the 1954 season, Harley-Davidson increased the flathead engine capacity to almost 900cc, in an attempt to close the performance gap between its flathead middleweight and the overhead-valve competition from across the pond. Neither the K nor the KH sold well. One problem was an old one: high price. At around $1,000, the middleweight Harleys were priced only 10 percent under the company's popular big overhead-valve Panheads. As the Sport model had proven in the 1920s, it was dangerous to price a middleweight so close to a heavyweight. But the K and KH pricing problems were especially damaging in the 1950s, because Harley now had serious competition from imported motorcycles.

ABOVE: Buoyed by the sales success of the E models, by 1948 Harley gave the more affordable WL similar styling features.

LEFT: Milwaukee motorcycle police officer Ray Schok, 1940s.

BY THE 1941 SEASON, KNUCKLEHEADS WERE OUTSELLING FLATHEAD BIG TWINS, SO THE EIGHTY WAS DROPPED TO AVOID COMPETING WITH THE NEW 1,200CC (74-CUBIC-INCH) OVERHEAD-VALVE MACHINES.

ABOVE: The original K model, introduced in 1952, was a direct response to the growing sales growth of imported bikes from England and Continental Europe.

LEFT: The K model was an all-new design based on unit construction—the crankcase and transmission shared the same housing.

ABOVE: By 1956, the K model engine's displacement had gone from 45 to 55 cubic inches. This was the last of this flathead engine; it was replaced the following year by the XL Sportster.

LEFT: TT racing river crossing, Minnesota, 1949.

A SEAMLESS CLOTH

After 1945, Harley-Davidson flatheads were few in comparison to the popular Harley overhead-valve Big Twins. But the Milwaukee flatheads were far more important to the company than mere numbers can convey. Harley-Davidson side-valve bikes kept the company going during the depths of the Great Depression. During World War II, some 80,000 Harley flatheads served the American and Allied forces, and kept the company's motorcycle building expertise at a high level. In the meek K and the better KH were the seeds that sprouted the Sportster. For Harley-Davidson, the flatheads were patterns on a seamless cloth called "evolution."

THE K AND KH PRICING PROBLEMS WERE ESPECIALLY DAMAGING IN THE 1950S, BECAUSE HARLEY NOW HAD SERIOUS COMPETITION FROM IMPORTED MOTORCYCLES.

CHAPTER 3

THE KNUCKLEHEAD ERA

BY GREG FIELD

A HUSH FELL THROUGH THE BALLROOM AS THE STAGE CURTAINS SLOWLY DREW BACK. DESPITE ALL THE HARDSHIPS BROUGHT BY THE GREAT DEPRESSION, HARLEY-DAVIDSON DEALERS FROM AS FAR AWAY AS JAPAN FILLED THE GREEN ROOM OF MILWAUKEE'S SCHROEDER HOTEL FOR THE FIRST DEALERS' CONVENTION IN FIVE YEARS.

Why go through all that bother when the cash-strapped company would likely unveil just another year's ration of minor updates and new paint colors to the stale and unpopular flatheads?

RUMORS. HINTS. SIGHTINGS. A BUZZ.

Through the dealer network, word had spread around the world that an all-new Harley-Davidson was ready to make its debut, a motorcycle so new, so bold, and so exciting that it would power the company and dealers into a full-throttle climb out of the Depression.

Chief Engineer William S. Harley and Harley promotions man "Hap" Jameson stood proudly on that stage, like two stone lions flanking a magnificent wrought-iron gate. I doubt anyone noticed them, however, because between them was what everyone had come to see.

Guys and gals outside the Milwaukee Motorcycle Club's clubhouse at Friess Lake, 1934. Backed by both Indian and Harley-Davidson and regulated by the American Motorcycle Association (AMA), the organized club scene exploded in the decade before World War II.

The hush deepened as the crowd absorbed every detail of the new machine. Even from the farthest corner of the room, dealers could see that the new motorcycle was a masterpiece of style—a bold fusion of art deco and streamlining that looked like a motorcycle, not another refinement of Harley's first motorized bicycles.

As the silence held for a long, enraptured moment, Bill Harley and the other company founders had to be wondering, "What are they all thinking?"

Seconds later, there was no doubt. From one corner came a whoop of triumph, followed by more, merging with wave after wave of applause. No one recorded whether Old Bill blushed, but certainly we could forgive him a little pride in his new baby's first standing ovation.

That bike was the Harley-Davidson Model E of 1936. The company liked to call its new machine the Sixty-One (in honor of its 61-cubic-inch displacement) or Overhead (in honor of its overhead valves, a first on a Harley production twin).

You and I know it today as the Knucklehead. That day was November 25, 1935, a defining moment in Harley-Davidson history that marked the real beginning of the Harley mystique. It was the day the Harley-Davidson Big Twin became more than just another motorcycle.

It was the day the legend began.

A CLOSER LOOK

After their first glimpse of the Sixty-One, the dealers impatiently sat through the rote presentation of the slightly revised flatheads that filled out the 1936 Harley line. The second it was over, they bum-rushed the stage to get a closer look at the Sixty-One.

ABOVE: Harley-Davidson opened a new chapter to its storied history when it launched the EL model in 1936. No doubt, this EL's wild colors drew a lot of attention!

BELOW: The appearance of H-D's 61 OHV model EL Knucklehead in 1936 set a new standard for high performance, reliability, and near perfect styling.

ABOVE: Not all 1930s riders were men. Margaret "Mugs" Pritchard of Appleton, Wisconsin, got her own 1932 Harley 45 model when she was just sixteen years old.

BELOW: The Model EL was the first production model to utilize an overhead-valve engine. To this day, all of Harley's Big Twin engines trace their DNA to that engine.

The sleek styling that was so evident from afar was even more striking at arm's length. The Sixty-One was a looker from any angle. Symmetry defined the new machine. Twin gas tanks straddled the frame's backbone tube, each with its own chrome-plated filler cap and petcock. A new instrument panel with a large, integral, 100-mile-per-hour speedometer (placed front and center, right where it would be easiest to read), an ammeter, an oil-pressure indicator, and the ignition switch bridged the gap between the tanks. Twin downtubes swept back from the steering head to the rear axle clips. The sweeping V of the cylinders, highlighted on the right side by the gleaming pushrod covers, framed the dramatic slash-cut chrome-plated air intake horn. Polished aluminum rocker housings, each with two round, chrome-plated covers over the ends of the rocker shafts, topped those cylinders.

The whole bike had a smooth, streamlined, almost organic look to it, each part so perfectly placed that it seemed the product of divine inspiration. Like the external changes that distinguish Neanderthal from modern man, the differences between VL and Knuckle were subtle but reflected important changes deep inside.

Surprisingly—at least from today's perspective—these great looks were the natural result of great engineering, rather than the result of after-the-fact styling by some industrial designer. In the 1930s, Harley didn't even have a formal styling department, let alone the services of someone like Willie G.

That's right, Harley fans. This was a time when Harley's engineers designed the best motorcycles they knew how to build and worried about what they looked like second. The looks evolved with the engineering. Under the leadership of cofounder and Chief Engineer William S. Harley, function determined form. Period. Contrast this approach with that used to design the Twin Cam six decades later.

ABOVE: The EL didn't earn its Knucklehead moniker until years later when it was replaced by the Panhead. Both names derive from the engines' respective rocker cover designs, one resembling knuckles, the other pans.

TOP LEFT: The early E models displaced 61 cubic inches. This 1937 EL sports a similar air intake horn as equipped on the 74- and 80-cubic-inch side-valve engines.

BOTTOM LEFT: Wide riding belts, breeches, high boots, peaked caps, and H-D wings marked the motorcycle look of the 1930s. Pictured left to right are Gary Koep, Leo Duffren, and Al Sharon at a Shawano rally in the 1930s.

Even the new bike's silhouette was right, shaped as it was by the dictates of function. At the time, nature's own teardrop was hailed as the aerodynamically perfect form. It's no accident then that the Knuckle's profile was defined by teardrop tanks superimposed over the teardrop loop of the frame, with wheels and a sprung seat tacked on. Look at a Softail today and you'll see the same perfect form.

The paint on the new machine accentuated its good looks. Gas tanks and fender crowns were blue; fender skirts, tank pinstripes, and wheel rims were white.

Peeking under the stylish gas tanks, dealers saw overhead valves and springs, promising that the new Sixty-One was more than just a pretty face. From what they could tell, about all the new engine had in common with the old flathead engine was the 45-degree V angle. They weren't far off in that assumption. The engine looked great too—all-gloss black iron, shiny aluminum, and gleaming chrome.

As they nodded approvingly, rumors circulated that the heads were the latest hemispherical type and that prototypes had already buried the needle on the 100-mile-per-hour speedo. Both rumors were true. (You didn't think the muscle cars of the 1950s and 1960s were the first hemis, did you?)

Mounted to the left tank, the shifter gate had five positions—1, N, 2, 3, and 4, front to rear. A four-speed! That was new too. And Harley pointed out that it was an advanced, constant-mesh design that was quieter, stronger, and more durable than the sliding-gear transmissions found on the competing Indian and foreign motorcycles.

Previous Harley frames had been all single-downtube types that were really just descendants of turn-of-the-century bicycle frames. On the Sixty-One, twin downtubes cradled the engine in a cage of rigid chrome-moly tubing. That frame and the beefy new springer front end promised handling to match the power.

ABOVE: Popular Milwaukee H-D dealer, Bill Knuth (seventh from left) outside the Milwaukee Motorcycle Club's headquarters before departing for a road run to the Shawano rally in 1939.

TOP LEFT: Since the 1910s, mechanics from around the world have been trained to properly service and repair Harley-Davidson motorcycles at the Milwaukee plant. Seen here is the Service School graduating class of 1937. Long-time Service Department manager Joe Ryan kneels at far right.

BOTTOM LEFT: What looks like a scene out of the 1954 film *The Wild One* actually took place outside of Milwaukee seventeen years before that Hollywood production was made. Milwaukee Motorcycle Club members negotiate a turn on a dirt road.

BELOW: Bikes were so simple and parts so interchangeable in the classic days that "Indian Joe Campbell" of Milwaukee kept a spare 80-inch side-valve engine that he swapped into this 61 OHV machine, 40EL1584. Campbell's nickname, "Indian Joe," came about when he once dared to ride an Indian motorcycle to his job as a frame builder at the Harley-Davidson factory. His pals there never let him forget it.

ABOVE: Brothers and rival dealers, Ray Tursky (H-D, front) and Erv Tursky (Indian, rear) at Lake Delton, Wisconsin, during a hillclimb in 1938. Bobbed fenders on these competition machines were copied by road riders who wanted their bikes to have the allure and glamour of a racer.

BELOW: Motorcycle rallies of the 1930s were family affairs where respectable behavior was encouraged and even kids attended wearing their own pint-size riding outfits.

Its swoopy new horseshoe-shaped oil tank filled the space under the seat. Its curved front contributed to the rounded, streamlined look of the new machine and hid the blocky battery from view. Savvy dealers noticed it had both feed and return tubes and knew what that meant: the Sixty-One's oiling system circulated oil through the engine and back to the oil tank to be used again. On previous Harleys the oil made a one-way trip through the engine and then dripped—"total loss" it was called.

In the Knucklehead, the dealers saw a knockout combination of cutting-edge looks and performance. It was, like the Model 94 Winchester or the Colt 1911 automatic pistol, an instant classic. It looked so right that it just had to work right. And like the Model 94 and the Colt pistol, the Knuckle's design indeed proved timeless, spawning whole industries of imitators.

One by one, the dealers filtered out of the ballroom with visions of the Sixty-One dancing in their heads.

DISAPPEARING ACT

After the curtains were closed on the stage that day, a curious thing happened: the most exciting new American motorcycle in over a decade disappeared completely, as if it had never been there at all.

For the rest of 1935 and early 1936, Harley insisted publicly that there was no Sixty-One. Harley's 1936 models were announced to the public in the January 1936 issue of *The Enthusiast*, and the Sixty-One was neither shown nor mentioned. Even the magazine's coverage of the dealers' convention ignored the Sixty-One.

Dealers knew better, but they were told to keep the secret because production would be "extremely limited" and that "under no circumstances should this model be ordered as a demonstrator!"

Why the secrecy when the dealers were so pumped and the market was so obviously ready?

Problems. Not big ones but messy ones nonetheless. The early Sixty-Ones didn't just leak oil, they gushed the slippery stuff.

For reasons unknown, Bill Harley had left out a return circuit for the oil pumped to the valves and rockers of his recirculating oil system. That oil ended up all over the engines and riders. Also, valve springs broke.

Thus, while dealers clamored for immediate delivery of the Sixty-One, Harley-Davidson denied the new bike's existence while simultaneously working on fixes for its problems and getting the factory geared up for full production. Harley's failure on the 1930 VL had been embarrassingly public. If it failed again on the Sixty-One, Harley wanted it to be a private failure this time.

Fortunately, about the same time the factory was ready, so were fixes for the engine. Harley solved the oiling problem by fitting individual enclosures and oil return lines for each valve. A switch to a new supplier solved the valve spring problem.

The first Sixty-One demonstrator models shipped in January 1936, still under the cloak of silence.

PUBLIC DEBUT

A month later, the Sixty-One began to blow its own cover by winning formal and informal races and the hearts of Harley fans everywhere. On February 2, Butch Quirk rode a sidecar-equipped Sixty-One to victory in a 350-mile endurance run sponsored by the Rose City Motorcycle Club of Portland, Oregon. Later in the month, the Graves & Chubbuck dealership in Pasadena, California, reported: "There has never been a motorcycle put out that has set the boys to talking so much as the Sixty-One. The news of

Fully enclosed valves greeted customers of the 1938 EL. Prior to that, the new OHV engine had partially exposed rocker arms that spattered oil onto the rider's legs.

BELOW: A premier collector bike today, this classic 1939 Knucklehead was just another entry in this endurance run held at Beaver Dam, Wisconsin, in 1941. Stuck in the mud, everyone along the route helped push to get it out.

ABOVE: One of H-D's more interesting classic machines was the model RLDR. Introduced in 1934 for Class C competition, this machine had racing parts in the engine but was otherwise fully street-legal. The idea was that a guy could ride his bike to the race, take off the lights and front fender, and then compete on the racetrack. Afterwards he would put the road parts back on and then ride his bike home again. In 1937 the RLDR was superceded by the WLDR model with a fully circulating oiling system. This example, 36RLDR2232, was owned by Adolph Roemer of Milwaukee, shown here with his girlfriend, Ethel Sentenne.

BELOW: Some prewar riders didn't make it back from World War II. One was Bud Waldman of Milwaukee, seen here on his first year Knucklehead, 36EL1740, at the Kenosha, Wisconsin, TT races held in 1937.

BELOW: Winter riding was a popular pastime, and Harley-Davidson offered a full line of winter accessories and gear. This view shows a 45-inch Harley flathead on Pewaukee Lake near Milwaukee in 1933.

ABOVE: Three riders toasting Bill Harley's great design masterpiece, the 1936 EL Knucklehead 61 OHV at Elkhart Lake in 1940. A little more than a year later after Pearl Harbor, many of these same guys would be in the armed forces and the carefree prewar party days would be over for the duration of the war.

BELOW: The commercial use of the motorcycle goes back to the origin of the device when doctors used them to make house calls. Later they were popular as delivery vehicles. The Gilmore Parcel Delivery service of Fond du Lac, Wisconsin, had a large fleet of sidecar package trucks in service before World War II.

its arrival was broadcast by the boys from the treetops, and five hours after its setup there was 120 miles on the speedometer."

All the rave reviews quickly eased the company's fears, so on February 21, Harley officially broke the silence and actually encouraged dealers to take orders for the Sixty-One. It also ran an ad for its new Big Twin in *The Motorcyclist*.

Harley offered the Sixty-One in two basic forms: the high-compression Model EL and medium-compression Model E. The base price was $380, but for that you didn't even get a jiffy stand! To get that, you had to pay another $14 for the Standard Solo Group. As an odd aside, Harley even offered the Knucklehead engine to midget-car racers as the 36EM.

Production models featured the same great looks as the prototype shown at the dealers' convention. In addition to the blue and white shown on the prototype, the order blanks listed four other color combinations. Some of these were downright gaudy, especially the Maroon with neon Nile Green panels and rims.

By March, orders for the Sixty-One rolled in faster than Harley-Davidson could build them, despite the ongoing Depression.

PROBLEMS, SOLUTIONS, AND A HAPPY ENDING

Unfortunately, the first Knuckleheads proved anything but trouble free. Certainly, the problems were nowhere near as serious as those of the first VLs, but they were serious enough that Bill Harley spent the next six months modifying part after part to refine the design. Some dealers expressed bitterness that once again the Motor Company used its customers as unpaid testers.

Those dealers were more right than they knew. A powerful combination of Harley-Davidson's need to quickly recoup the bike's high development costs, the financial squeeze of the Depression, and labor laws that prevented H-D engineers from working overtime forced company management into releasing the design before it was fully mature. In fact, it was so immature, you could call the 1936 Sixty-Ones mass-produced prototypes or beta versions in the parlance of the Internet age.

Fortunately, the problems that resulted weren't as severe as those that plagued the early VLs.

Improvements, rather than innovations, earmark the overhead-valve Big Twin for 1939. Among the EL's improvements were modified clutch and transmission designs for smoother shifting.

  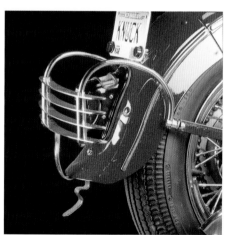

TOP: This 1939 EL boasts added chromed parts and a two-person buddy seat.

BOTTOM LEFT: The fishtail muffler had become a mainstay during the 1930s. This EL has its muffler and muffler tip chrome plated.

BOTTOM CENTER: The springer fork is among the identifiable features of a Knucklehead model. Most springer front ends were painted, unlike this custom chrome-plated fork.

BOTTOM RIGHT: Helping to underscore the art deco trend, this rear bumper on a 1939 EL helped protect the "tombstone" taillight.

The features that made the Sixty-One engine so exciting also proved the most troublesome. Its oil pump was more than adequate to pump oil all the way to the new OHV (overhead-valve mechanism), but adjustment of the oil supply to each rocker arm was critical—and the standardized factory adjustment left some bikes with problems from over-oiled or under-oiled valves.

The consequences of over-oiling were unpleasant but not catastrophic: blue clouds of oil smoke and oil all over the bike and the rider's legs. Some even used more oil than the previous Harleys with total-loss oil systems.

If the adjustment erred on the side of under-oiling, the consequences were much more serious, ranging from what Harley described as "squeaking" valves to rapid and excessive wear of the valves, rockers, and shafts.

For each of these problems and dozens more, the company quickly came up with fixes. During the year, Bill Harley modified nearly every part at least once, and some he modified three or more times before getting them right. All that is testament to his determination to make the Sixty-One's performance as good as it looked.

Dealers and riders may have griped, but they bought Sixty-Ones anyway. They overlooked all of the model's problems because its over OHV engine gave it unprecedented performance for an American production twin. Even in its mild stock state of tune, the OHV engine could propel the Sixty-One to an honest 95 miles per hour. With a little work, it easily outran its 100-mile-per-hour speedometer.

And unlike the flatheads from both Harley and Indian, the new OHV could sustain those high speeds indefinitely. Not only was it the best-looking bike on the planet, it was among the fastest. Of its US-built contemporaries, only the Crocker held a clear advantage.

Harley's original plan was to build and sell 1,600 overheads that first year. By the time the plant switched over to 1937 production in the fall of 1936, it had actually sold between 1,700 and 1,900 of the expensive new model, depending on whose records you believe.

ABOVE: In 1941, competition star Tommy Hayes of Dallas, Texas, was voted the most popular rider in the United States of America. A few weeks earlier Hayes and another rider had been killed on the racetrack at Oakland, California.

LEFT: Some early Knuckleheads like this 1939 example soldiered on as daily street rides into the 1980s. The Knucklehead could reliably maintain highway speeds if you didn't mind a little vibration, dripping oil, and if a guy routinely tightened all the nuts and bolts on his machine.

It wasn't until 1941 that the overhead-valve Big Twin received a boost in displacement to 74 cubic inches. That became known as the FL model. This 1941 is an EL, but both models look the same.

Yes, Harley's flathead Big Twins did outsell the Sixty-One that year, but everyone knew the Overhead would soon take over.

It was a fitting start to the legend.

1937: THE KNUCKLEHEAD TAKES OVER

If the original Sixty-One was the "beta" Big Twin, the 1937 version was the ready-for-prime-time Knuckle Version 1.0. It came with a beefier frame, larger rear brake, 120-mile-per-hour speedometer, and more improvements than you care to know about. What matters is that it really was improved, and that it sold even better than before.

And the Sixty-One left its mark on the whole Harley line that year. All the other flathead models were dressed up in Sixty-One style and were fitted with recirculating oil systems. In addition, the Big-Twin flatties got the four-speed transmission and dual-cradle frame.

It was time to break some records with Harley's hot rod. On March 13, Joe Petrali, who had helped Bill Harley design the Sixty-One, piloted a specially prepared Knuckle to a straightaway record of 136.183 miles per hour on the sand of Daytona Beach.

On April 8 and 9, a true iron man named Fred Ham took a couple days off from his job as a Pasadena motorcycle cop to assault the record for the most miles ridden in twenty-four hours. To complicate matters, he planned to do all the riding himself on a stock Sixty-One he'd purchased in October 1936. First, he laid out a 5-mile course on Murac Dry Lake (the sight of Edwards Air Force Base today). Then, with the help of a crew of twenty, oil flares to light the course at night, and quarts of cold milk to keep him energized, Ham proceeded to go 'round and 'round for twenty-four straight hours, stopping only for gas and to change the chain. In all, he rode 1,825 miles, averaging 76.6 miles per hour, a new record.

ABOVE: This 1940 EL has the classic post seat that moves up and down on a pogolike hydraulic damper system. That and the 16-inch balloon tires helped smooth the ride for the rigid-frame bike.

LEFT: Ray Tursky's Madison, Wisconsin, salesroom and parts counter was a model Harley-Davidson dealership in the late 1950s. The newly introduced XL model Sportster is seen in foreground.

ABOVE: With the introduction of the 74 OHV model FL Knucklehead in 1941, Harley riders now had a high-speed, all-around motorcycle of unsurpassed good looks and great durability. Many modern H-D styling and engineering features are based on this landmark machine.

BELOW: Mel Krueger crashes a board wall at the Wausau Motorcycle Rodeo in 1936. Daredevil events like this one were once popular entertainment at motorcycle gatherings.

In other news, Harley-Davidson production workers voted to unionize in March 1937, which broke the heart of founder and company production chief Bill Davidson. Some believe the struggle against unionization contributed to his quick decline and death on April 21.

1938: "SMOOTHER, QUIETER, CLEANER"

After all the changes of 1936 and 1937, the Knucklehead was a mature design. Harley's theme for the 1938 Knuckleheads was "smoother, quieter, cleaner." It was time to make the Knuckle more civilized.

The biggest change was a set of new valve covers that completely enclosed the rockers and valves, keeping the oil in and the dirt out. Black pants were no longer mandatory.

For 1939, the changes were mostly cosmetic, including the change to what is perhaps the prettiest two-tone paint scheme ever used on a Harley. Even so, Knuckle sales were way up for the year, while sales of the flatheads were stagnant or declining.

THE BIG-PORT KNUCKLEHEAD, FL, AND WORLD WAR II

Even with war breaking out in Europe, Harley restyled the Sixty-One for 1940, with new sheet metal and tank badges, half-moon footboards, and the option of fat 16-inch tires. Park a 1940 Knuckle next to a Heritage Springer, and I guarantee you'll see the resemblance. The engine got more powerful and more reliable too, courtesy of larger intake ports, manifold, and carburetor, along with a beefier bottom end and clutch.

By 1941, American industry was gearing up for war. Harley was too, but the company's engineers still found time to bore and stroke their OHV engine to 74 cubic inches, creating the Model FL engine, known as the Seventy-Four Overhead to distinguish it from the regular Seventy-Four, which was a flathead. They threw in an all-new clutch too, to handle the extra torque of the big FL.

By the time the 1942 models began rolling off the line in early fall of 1941, America was perilously close to entering the war. American factories were churning out planes, tanks, guns, and other military equipment, to the exclusion of almost everything else. And so was Harley-Davidson. With fat contracts to build bikes for US and Allied forces and shortages of steel, copper, iron, and aluminum, Harley-Davidson only promised each dealer one new bike for the 1942 model year.

Then came December 7 and the attack on Pearl Harbor. On January 1, 1942, all production of civilian cars, trucks, and motorcycles was halted for the duration of the war. For most of the war years, you had to be a policeman, fireman, essential war worker, or senator's son to get a new Harley.

Those dealers who joined up or were drafted had to worry about keeping their hides whole, while those left behind worried about staying in business. It was a struggle.

While the rest of the country mourned casualties of war, Harley suffered its own. On February 7, 1942, Harley-Davidson President Walter Davidson Sr. died. William H. Davidson, son of the late founder William A., soon took his uncle's place at the head of the company. He would lead the company for the next forty-one years.

In May 1942, gasoline and sugar rationing began in the United States. Worse yet, aluminum became "unobtainium." To get pistons to repair a customer's bike, Harley dealers had to send in the wrecked ones so they could be melted down to build replacements.

To help its dealers stay in business, Harley steered them toward the only sales the government allowed: cop bikes. Dealer bulletins even made suggestions about

TOP: With the conclusion of World War II, Harley-Davidson got back to the business of building bikes for America's citizens. This 1946 EL was among the first to hit the road in postwar America.

BOTTOM LEFT: The Knucklehead engine, with its massive rocker covers, is considered a classic design among motorcycle enthusiasts everywhere.

BOTTOM CENTER: Chromium was still a scarce commodity after World War II, which explains why many of the initial postwar bikes were composed primarily of painted parts.

BOTTOM RIGHT: The simplicity of the rigid frame is a favorite for custom bike builders today. The locking tool box was an accessory that, like the EL's frame, has found its place in today's custom bike market too.

BELOW: In front of Bill Knuth's H-D shop in Milwaukee, Wisconsin, 1949.

ABOVE: Sunglasses go well with a 1961 OHV.

BELOW: You didn't have to be an outlaw to ride a motorcycle in the early days, but it helped.

the perfect Christmas gift to buy the local police chief. Of course, that gift had the Harley logo!

For 1943, Harley built 27,000 military motorcycles, but only about 200 Knuckles. These were civilian or police bikes, but there were a few attempts to dress the Overhead in olive drab. Harley even experimented with joining two Knucklehead motors together to power a light tank for the Canadian army. A true War War Hog, eh?

On September 18, 1943, Harley-Davidson cofounder and Chief Engineer Bill Harley died.

By 1944, restrictions on civilian sales were loosened to allow the sale of more than 500 Knuckles. The government also surplused many thousands of military motorcycles, and Harley dealers snapped them up and quickly sold them to their eager customers.

By the start of 1945, the battles raged on, but the Allies were confident victory was at hand. The Germans surrendered on May 8, and Japan followed on September 2.

PICKING UP THE PIECES

At the start of the 1946 model year, opportunities abounded for Harley-Davidson and its dealers. The war was won, the boys were coming home by the thousands, and demand was high because most prewar motorcycles were worn out or scrapped for lack of spares during the wartime years. Time for Harley and the dealers to cash in.

Even better, the flagship of Harley's motorcycle fleet—the Knucklehead—was still the best and most technologically advanced American production motorcycle. Ten years after the Knuckle's introduction, Indian was still peddling flatheads and was rapidly losing market share to the more advanced Harley Overheads.

As a result, Harley-Davidson was able to sell all the motorcycles it could find raw materials to build. Harley built 6,746 Knuckleheads for 1946, more than for any preceding year. The same was true for 1947. After twelve years of production, the Knucklehead was still the American champion.

ABOVE: Indicative of an early customized Harley, this 1947 FL sports many features not found on a stock model.

BELOW: Near Holy Hill outside of Milwaukee, Wisconsin, 1950.

ABOVE: Among the EL's favored styling cues are the round air intake bell, tombstone taillight, springer fork, and post-mounted pogo seat.

BELOW: A red 1947 EL parked in the snow in front of a tall evergreen. It's beginning to look a lot like Christmas!

THEY'RE ALL KNUCKLEHEADS

By November 1947, the champion got a facelift. Harley released its 1948 lineup, including what it called the "biggest motorcycle story of the year," a new version of the Overhead engine to carry the company into the future. The most obvious change was new valve covers that looked like chrome-plated cake pans. The real story was under the pans, however. Aluminum heads and hydraulic lifters made Harley's OHV motor smoother, quieter, more oil tight, cooler running, and more maintenance free, if not more powerful. In time, it was given the nickname "Panhead."

For 1966, Harley's Overhead was given yet another facelift. It, too, was a top-end job that made the Overhead smoother, quieter, more oil tight, cooler running, and more maintenance free than its predecessor but not much lighter or more powerful. Enthusiasts soon christened it "Shovelhead."

In 1984 came yet another revision to Harley's OHV, called the V2 Evolution engine. With aluminum cylinders and many other updates, the Evo was a thoroughly modern fulfillment of Bill Harley's original design. When combined with a restyled and updated chassis in new models such as the Softail and FLHT, the Evolution engine once again gave Harley-Davidson's Big Twin true mass-market appeal. As a result, by the early 1990s, the once-ailing Milwaukee firm would again achieve the same dominance in the American marketplace that it had enjoyed at the end of the Knuckle's reign.

For 1999, the all-new Twin Cam 88 eclipsed the Evo, and the evolutionary line that began with the 1936 Knuckle came to an end. But after sixty-plus years of change, during which Harley engineers made thousands of refinements, the basics that made the 1936 Sixty-One engine so appealing remained unchanged.

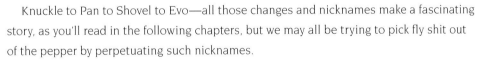

Knuckle to Pan to Shovel to Evo—all those changes and nicknames make a fascinating story, as you'll read in the following chapters, but we may all be trying to pick fly shit out of the pepper by perpetuating such nicknames.

Truth is, the switch from Knucklehead to Panhead was barely noticed by most riders—and it wasn't accompanied by a nickname change. That came years later. To Harley-Davidson and to Harley riders, the new engines were still just Sixty-One and Seventy-Four Overheads. After the Shovel came along, such names were finally useful, and when the Evo came along, even Harley got in on the name game.

Nevertheless, when enthusiasts born during Harley's second century look back on all this, fine distinctions that seem so important to the story of Harley's first century—Panhead, Shovelhead, Evolution, and even Twin Cam—will likely be forgotten.

From the viewpoint of centuries, all those bleed into one. They're all just incremental updates of the original Sixty-One engine.

In other words, they're all Knuckleheads.

CHAPTER 4

THE PANHEAD ERA

BY GREG FIELD

DESPITE THE THOUSANDS OF US SOLDIERS KILLED IN WORLD WAR II, AMERICA'S JUBILATION KNEW NO BOUNDS IN THE FALL OF 1945. THE ALLIES HAD SOUNDLY TROUNCED HITLER AND TOJO, THE COUNTRY'S HEROES WERE ON THEIR WAY HOME, AND AMERICA GLOWED WITH PRIDE THAT IT HAD PROVEN ITSELF THE WORLD'S NEW SUPERPOWER.

From Harley-Davidson's boardroom, the sunrise of the postwar era looked glorious. Spurred on by military sales, the company had revitalized and retooled itself to build nearly 100,000 copies of "The Motorcycle That Won the War." Harley-Davidson was ready to best all previous production records.

And the market for Harley's Big Twins looked as limitless as the Lake Michigan horizon stretching easy from Milwaukee. Millions of servicemen—including thousands of former Harley-mounted dispatch riders—were suddenly discharged, their wallets fat with money they couldn't spend at the front and their sense of adventure honed keen by war. On the home front, after years of sacrifice, gas rationing, reduced speed limits, and tire shortages, gearheads couldn't wait to cash in their war bonds and drive, drive, drive, in rapid pursuit of the good life.

ABOVE: Self-adjusting hydraulic valves, capped with new rocker covers, highlighted the improvements for 1948's Model FL. The engine eventually became known as the Panhead.

LEFT: This 1948 FL looks stout and regal with its centerstand down. This bike boasts more chrome than what most bikes had in 1948.

There's no denying that this is a police bike! With Indian out of the picture in 1954, police departments relied solely on Harley-Davidson for their patrol bikes.

Unfortunately, that postwar sunrise quickly darkened for Harley-Davidson. New clouds of war rolled in from the east, as the Soviet Union tightened its stranglehold on Eastern Europe and Mao's Communist forces marched toward victory in China. The terms "Iron Curtain" and "Cold War" gained everyday usage, and Harley-Davidson was once again called on to sacrifice.

The US government's first volley in the Cold War was the Marshall Plan. Implemented to contain the Soviets by rebuilding the war-ravaged economies of Europe and England, the Marshall Plan sent hundreds of millions of dollars in scarce raw materials, such as steel and chromium, overseas to America's economic competitors.

At the same time, drastically lowered import duties enabled those competitors to ship back goods and undercut US manufacturers, including Harley-Davidson. While the Marshall Plan may have contained Communism abroad, it was a one-two punch that hindered capitalism at home—especially in Milwaukee.

As a result of getting only a fraction of the steel, chrome, aluminum, and rubber it needed, Harley-Davidson couldn't build enough Knuckleheads in 1946 and 1947 to meet the demand. Think waiting lists for new Harleys began in the 1990s? Think again! Guys who wanted a new Harley in the late 1940s often had to wait. Those who didn't want to wait looked to the other makers.

Only one group of makers had a seemingly limitless supply of new bikes to offer.

THE BRITISH INVASION

While the US government was reining in Harley-Davidson, the British government put the spurs to its motorcycle industry by forcing it to export 75 percent of its output or face reduced quotas of the same scarce materials denied Harley.

Only the United States had the cash to buy all those Brit bikes, and because of the reduced tariffs that were part of the Marshall Plan, those machines were artificially cheap. They were also light, fast, and fun, and there weren't enough Harleys to go around. Instead of the trickle of Triumphs and Nortons that had been imported before the war, 1946 brought a flood of British machinery. England exported nearly 10,000 motorcycles to the United States in 1946 and more than 15,000 in 1947. Many, if not most of those motorcycles, were sold to potential Harley customers.

Imagine the great frustration in Milwaukee. After barely surviving the Great Depression and helping win the war, Harley-Davidson was stabbed in the back by governmental policy. Did the company pout or cry foul, or scream, "That's not fair?" Nope. Those tactics would come later.

Harley chose to compete. That doesn't mean the company's engineers immediately countered the British threat with like machines. That, too, came later, with the launch of the K models and Sportsters. In the late 1940s, Harley ceded the performance market to the British and steered its Big Twin line down a new road, one that led not to a lighter weight or greater performance, but nonetheless to refinement and success.

That more-refined Big Twin made its debut in the fall of 1947, for the 1948 model year. At first glance, the 1948 Sixty-One and Seventy-Four Overheads didn't look very new. In

AS A RESULT OF GETTING ONLY A FRACTION OF THE STEEL, CHROME, ALUMINUM, AND RUBBER IT NEEDED, HARLEY-DAVIDSON COULDN'T BUILD ENOUGH KNUCKLEHEADS IN 1946 AND 1947 TO MEET THE DEMAND.

This FL could easily be a rolling advertisement for the many optional accessories available to owners in 1957.

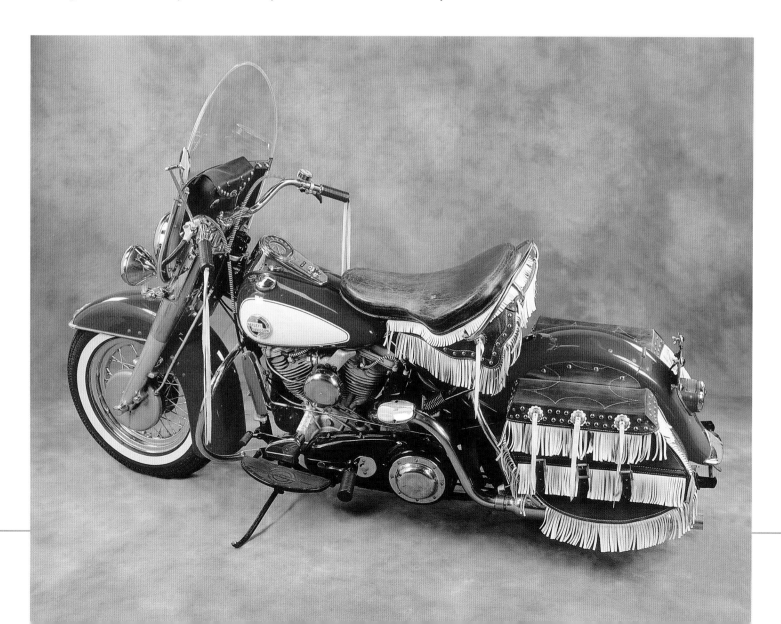

ABOVE: The Hydra-Glide FL was launched in 1948. The name derived from the hydraulic-damped front fork. This 1956 FL boasts accessories and unique tank graphics.

BELOW: Display put on by Milwaukee Motorcycle Club and dealer Bill Knuth, 1949. Note early model.

fact, nothing was really new, except the whole top end of the engine. But what a difference a new top end can make.

Most noticeable were the curious new valve covers that looked like chrome-plated cake pans atop each cylinder head. Though Harley didn't even have a name for the new model, Harley enthusiasts soon began referring to it as the "Panhead."

THE PANHEAD MOTOR

With a bulletproof bottom end and decent power, the last of the Knucklehead engines were the equal of all but the most exotic of their contemporaries. Still, they leaked too much oil and were prone to overheating when pushed hard, so Harley engineers applied to the Harley Big Twin some of the lessons learned in the wartime pressure cooker about making air-cooled motors more reliable.

One of those lessons was that aluminum alloy was a better choice of material for the cylinder heads than iron. Aluminum gets rid of engine heat much better than iron, and it is lighter too. Harley had known all this long before the war (and had even used aluminum heads on some of its flathead motors) but had stuck with iron because aluminum was comparatively expensive. That is, it was more expensive until thousands and thousands of surplus planes were flown home after the war and melted down into light, shiny aluminum ingots. When it began to look as if aluminum would be cheap and plentiful in postwar America, H-D took advantage of the opportunity and used the material for the Panhead.

The new aluminum cylinder heads for the Panhead were completely redesigned to make the whole engine tidier and more reliable. Harley engineers eliminated external oil lines by adding internal passages to oil the cylinders and heads. The valvetrain was redesigned for greater longevity and reduced maintenance, and the aforementioned

chrome-plated pans enclosed the resulting assembly. The new covers lent a simple, more modern look to the new heads—and they kept the oil in and dirt out far better than the Knucklehead's separate covers.

Another surprise lurked under those pans, however: hydraulic lifters!

Before the Panhead was introduced, OHV motorcycle engines had purely mechanical links between the cam lobes in the bottom end and the valves in the heads. This simple and effective system required frequent and diligent adjustment to hold the clackity clacking of loose valves at bay and prevent the heartbreak of burned valves. Nevertheless, valve adjustments were a maintenance hassle that nobody really needed.

Hydraulic lifters solved all those problems by automatically adjusting themselves for proper clearances. Harley engineers put one of them atop each Panhead pushrod. After initial adjustment at the factory, the lifters required adjustment only after major engine repair. Hydraulic lifters meant less time wrenching, so the owner of the new Panhead could spend more time riding. It didn't hurt that the new lifters made the engine quieter, so the rider could better enjoy the music of the exhaust note.

The Panhead wasn't the first engine with hydraulic lifters, but what mattered to the company was that the Panhead was the first *motorcycle* engine with hydraulic lifters, and that they worked, which they did . . . except when they didn't. We'll get to that later.

Harley took its Big Twin in a new direction with the Panhead. Instead of spending scarce development money to make more powerful motorcycles to compete with hot rod British twins, Harley-Davidson concentrated on making its big Overheads quieter, more oil tight, and easier to maintain so they would appeal to a broader cross section of Americans. With the 1948 Panhead, Harley's OHV Big Twin began a long rumble down a new byway. The new Panhead was one small step for motorcycling but one giant step for the company. It was also the start of the most innovative era in Harley history.

ABOVE: The Hydra-Glide's final year was 1957. The following year Harley replaced the dated rigid frame with a chassis that included rear shock absorbers.

BELOW: In 1950 the clean-cut AMA club look was still being promoted by Harley-Davidson as this Big Twin Hydra-Glide ad demonstrates.

THE WHOLE BIKE WAS RESTYLED IN A BOLD, MODERN (FOR 1949) FASHION THAT WAS AS DIFFERENT FROM THE OLD SPRINGER-FORKED BIKES AS THE FIRST KNUCKLEHEAD WAS FROM THE OLD FLATHEAD IT REPLACED.

The FL, now known as the Duo-Glide, had a whole new profile for 1958. The twin rear shock absorbers altered the looks—and ride—dramatically.

HYDRA-GLIDING INTO THE FIFTIES

Nineteen forty-one was the on-ramp to the paranoid, but prosperous, 1950s. Lines drawn around the world that year culminated in several bloody Cold War skirmishes. Pizza fever began its spread to the heartland. Television began its rise toward becoming the new national pastime. Bikini bathing suits shocked and titillated swimmers across America. The 33⅓-rpm, long-play record was introduced, and Polaroid's new Land camera began spoiling Americans with photographs that self-developed in sixty seconds. Roller derby put pro wrestling on wheels, the first Volkswagen "bugs" hit America's shores, and America's first prefabricated suburb rose out of a Long Island field. And George Orwell's prophetic novel, 1984, was published to critical acclaim.

It's no surprise that the bike that came to define American motorcycling for the 1950s also made its entrance in 1949: a vastly updated and restyled Panhead, eventually called the Hydra-Glide.

This time, the differences between old and new were anything but subtle. The whole bike was restyled in a bold, modern (for 1949) fashion that was as different from the old springer-forked bikes as the first Knucklehead was from the old flathead it replaced. And the more modern look of the Hydra-Glide was as timeless as that of the Knucklehead that preceded it. Compare one to today's Heritage Softail, and you'll find a lot more similarities than differences. In many ways, the Hydra-Glides were the classic Pans.

Most noticeable was the all-new front end, dominated by massive-looking telescopic forks. Harley-Davidson named its innovative new hydraulic forks Hydra-Glides. Before long, the Panheads themselves became known by the Hydra-Glide moniker, and Harley-Davidson encouraged the trend by offering optional front-fender badges featuring the name.

Why telescopic forks when the old spring fork had worked so well for so long? Because, truthfully, springers hadn't worked that well at all—they had a mere 2 inches of travel and needed constant maintenance—and because most of the competition had already switched to telescopic forks. BMW built the world's first production motorcycle with a

Continued on page 105

TOP: This 1959 FLH includes an optional air horn for helping clear the road ahead.
BOTTOM LEFT: The Panhead engine is a thing of beauty.
BOTTOM RIGHT: Highway light bars have always been a favorite of Harley owners. This light bar, perched on the fork of a 1959 FLH, resemble what's found on today's Road King.

HUMMERS, SCATS, AND TOPPERS: THE MILWAUKEE TWO-STROKES

By Greg Field

To the winner go the spoils. Among the spoils of World War II was a 125cc two-stroke engine from German maker DKW.

Harley-Davidson, as a member of the winning side, claimed that engine as part of Germany's wartime reparation. Harley put the little two-stroke engine into production for midyear 1948 as the Model S, a fun little bike with a girder-type front suspension, rigid rear, and a little "peanut" tank that later charmed the world on the XLCH Sportster. It was Harley's best seller that year, with more than 10,000 units trailing blue smoke out dealership doors.

In 1951, Harley updated the Model S with a telescopic fork. That fork was of the male-slider type, like all the "upside-down" forks on the latest Buells. In 1953, Harley punched the engine out to a 165cc and called it the ST. In 1954, Harley added a second model, the STU, which was fitted with a carburetor restrictor to reduce power to under 5 horsepower, so the kiddies could ride them on the street without a license. In 1955 came a third model, a stripper with the old 125 engine and a squeeze-bulb-type bicycle horn as stock equipment. Harley called its new kiddy bike the Hummer. It didn't need a restrictor, because its little engine was only good for 3 horsepower.

With the invasion of light, powerful Brit bikes in the early 1950s, sales of the Harley two-strokes steadily declined. Then, came another invasion—an invasion of scooters from Italy— that cut further into sales for Harley's lightweights.

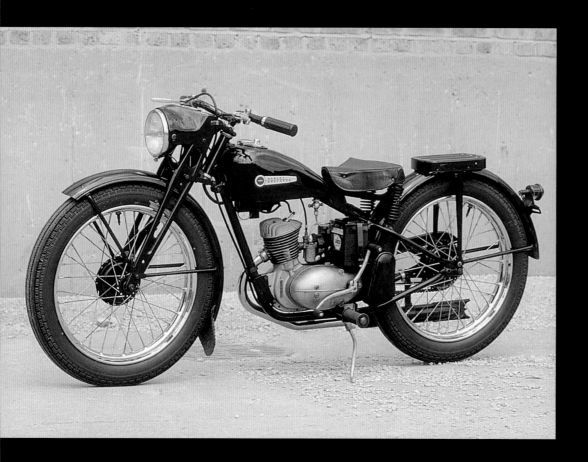
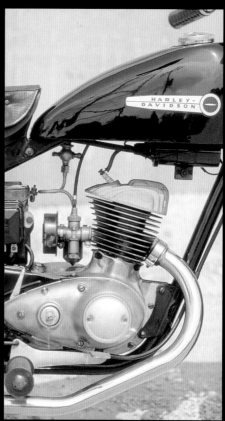

The Hummer was one of Harley's third attempts to reach the booming youth market following World War II.

LEFT: The Topper was Harley's failed attempt to cash in on the scooter boom.

BELOW: The Hummer made up in style what it lacked in speed.

ABOVE: 1965 Hummer.

ABOVE: 1971 Baja.

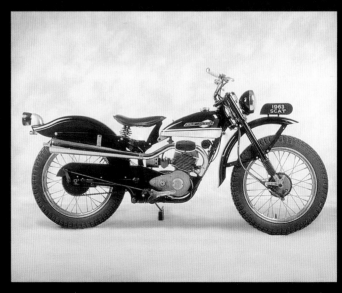

ABOVE: 1963 Scat.

ABOVE: 1972 Shortster.

Harley fought back on the scooter front. The battlewagon of Milwaukee's 1960 counterattack was the all-new Model A Topper scooter. Where the Italian scooters were sleek, light, and zippy, the Topper was slab-sided, heavy, and underpowered, with only about 5 horsepower. For 1961, Harley hot-rodded the Topper to keep up with the Lambrettas and Vespas. The brawny Topper H came with almost twice the horsepower, but by then the scooter craze was played out, and everyone had moved on to small motorcycles from Japan. Sales declined, and the Topper was discontinued in 1965.

For 1962, Harley punched out its two-stroke engine to 175cc for use on the Pacer street bike and Scat dual sport, or "scrambler," as such bikes were called at the time. Harley did this in an attempt to give its two-stroke bikes enough power to keep up with the more modern lightweights from Japan and from Harley's Aermacchi affiliate. For 1963, Harley finally gave the Pacers and Scats rear suspension. And what a suspension! As on the later Softail models and Buells, Harley hid the suspension components under the transmission. For 1966, the new Bobcat replaced the Pacer and Scat. The Bobcat was clothed in fiberglass, with its gas tank and boat-tail rear section made from the material.

At the end of 1966, Harley discontinued the little Bobcat and used the full capacity of its Milwaukee plants to build the more profitable Electra Glides and Sportsters.

The Hummers, Scats, Toppers, and the rest were good little bikes but were never really accepted by Harley's hardcore riders and dealers.

Continued from page 98

hydraulically damped telescopic fork in 1935, and by 1949, the design had become the industry standard for front suspension design. Harley knew that another tidal wave of Brit bikes with telescopic forks was about to wash over America's shores, so the Panhead needed an immediate suspension and image upgrade to keep from being swept aside.

The Panhead got telescopic forks, but it got a set that could only have come from Milwaukee. Unlike the spindly looking forks on the foreign bikes, the Hydra-Glide forks looked stout and muscular. The fork legs were spaced wide to clear the fat front tire and the new front fender. The upper tubes and whole top of the fork assembly were shrouded in black-painted, stamped-steel cover panels that gave the front end the massive good looks that are still so much a part of Harley style. Polished stainless-steel covers were optional, but the bright covers looked so good that few bikes were ordered with the plain-Jane black ones.

Ads for the 1949 Panhead emphasized that the new forks were not just about looks, however. "Hydra-Glide sets a new standard in smooth-as-flying, road-hugging comfort," said one, and the ad copy was right. Hydra-Glide forks gave more than twice the travel of the springer forks and their velocity-sensitive valving tamed bumpy roads much better than the old springers. Along with the new fork came a much larger and more powerful front brake.

With its shiny Panhead motor and hydraulic forks, the Hydra-Glide was definitely not Grandpa's old Silent Gray Fellow, or flathead, or Knuckle for that matter. It set a new standard for touring bikes of its era, and it was faster, smoother, better handling, and more mannered than any Harley that had come before.

FOOT SHIFT

Though the Hydra-Glide set a new standard for touring bikes of its era, its foot clutch and hand shift made it seem a prewar relic. All the latest machines from Britain had foot shifters, and the feature was seen as an essential component of a postwar pedigree. Even Indian outshifted Harley on this one, fitting a few Chiefs with foot shifters in late 1949 and early 1950. After swimming against the flow for too long, Harley introduced foot shift as a Panhead option in late 1951.

Still, Harley's management knew that many of its customers were die-hard traditionalists, so they offered the customer a choice of foot shift or hand shift. Most of them wanted foot shift, and by 1954, foot-shifted bikes outsold hand-shifted machines by a margin of nearly two to one. That margin continued to widen every year until only a few hand-shift models were produced each year in the late 1960s.

The Panhead motor itself got a small-but-important update in 1953. In a successful attempt to make the hydraulic lifters more reliable, Harley engineers moved them from the top of the pushrods to the bottom, closer to the oil pump. With this small change, the Panhead's lifters were truly reliable at last. And the basics of this lifter scheme remained in use through the end of the Evolution engines.

Although today the factory celebrates 1903 as its first year, Harley designated 1954 its 50th Anniversary. To mark the occasion, all 1954 Harleys featured special 50th Anniversary badges on their front fenders.

OPPOSITE: The FLHF designation for this 1960 model denotes that it has a high-compression engine and foot shifter. Hand shifters were still in use during the 1960s.

BELOW: Employees of Harley-Davidson's Experimental Department outside the factory front door, circa 1950. These unsung heroes were the guys who developed and tested new components and motorcycles devised in H-D's Engineering Department. They helped build and maintain the famous Harley-Davidson legacy of today.

WITH ITS SHINY PANHEAD MOTOR AND HYDRAULIC FORKS, THE HYDRA-GLIDE WAS DEFINITELY NOT GRANDPA'S OLD SILENT GRAY FELLOW, OR FLATHEAD, OR KNUCKLE FOR THAT MATTER.

ABOVE: New dual-point/dual-fire ignition systems were among improvements for 1961. This FLF also showcases some of the accessory options for the year too.

BELOW: H-D Service School instructor John Nowak listens to an engine in 1960.

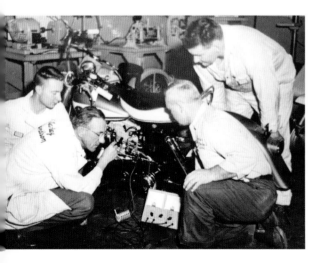

In December 1953, as the 1954 models were rolling off the production line in earnest, H-D's image took a real drubbing in the sensationalist biker flick *The Wild One*. The movie begins with the warning: "This is a shocking story. It could never take place in most American towns—but it did in this one. It is a public challenge not to let it happen again."

Though the bikers in the movie seem almost wholesome now—and their antics in taking over the town probably wouldn't rate a disorderly conduct charge today—the movie really shocked audiences in 1953 and 1954. No longer did the America public think of a motorcycle club as a group of uniformed Shriners riding full-dress Harleys in the Fourth of July parade. A club was now seen as a bunch of unshaven, drunken rowdies, as typified by Marlon Brando's *Wild One* gang, the Black Rebels MC. Worse yet, the film's villains—Chino (played by Lee Marvin) and his club—rode Harleys and Indians, while Brando's anti-hero Johnny and his group rode Triumphs. After *The Wild One*—and a whole slew of Hollywood imitation—America had a new idea of what kind of people they'd meet on a Harley.

For 1955, Harley-Davidson released its own "Wild One"—the FLH Super Sport. The "H" stood for "high compression." That higher compression, combined with ported and polished intakes, boosted FLH horsepower by 10 percent. This extra power helped haul the weight of all the chrome gadgets and touring gear that riders were starting to bolt onto their Hydra-Glides. Bottom ends on all the 1955 Pan engines were beefed up with stout Timken tapered bearings in place of the old roller bearings.

For 1956, the FLH was given even more guts, courtesy of the hot new "Victory" camshaft and even higher compression pistons. Also part of the package was a bold FLH decal on each side of the oil tank, announcing to all that this was Harley's hot rod. For 1957, not much changed on the Big Twins, because Harley saved all the glory for its new Sportster.

So ended the Hydra-Glide line. During eight years of production, the King of Bikes— or at least the bike of the King (Elvis bought a tarted-up 1957 Hydra-Glide)—gained weight, power, better lifters, and a stronger bottom end. What it really needed was rear suspension. That would be the headline feature of the Hydra-Glide's successor, the 1958 Duo-Glide.

ABOVE: By 1962, the Duo-Glide was a mainstay among the touring-bike crowd. This FLH, dressed with hard saddlebags and tall windshield, is ready to chase the horizon.

BELOW: Few Indians and foreign bikes are visible at this motorcycle parking area at the Cedarburg, Wisconsin, races around 1950. English bikes would become more common as the 1950s progressed, while once great Indian went extinct.

ENTER THE DUO-GLIDE

While rigid frames and sprung seats provided all the rear suspension anyone expected when the Knucklehead was introduced in the 1930s, the Panhead's hardtail rear end was an antiquated design by the late 1950s. Even the out-sized saddlebags and crash bars riders fitted to many Hydra-Glides could no longer hide the lack of rear suspension. Worse yet, the new Sportster of 1957 had rear suspension, as had its predecessors, the models K and KH. How come the lesser twins had rear suspension while the King of the Highway was still a hardtail? Big Twin riders rightfully felt left out. That is until the fall of 1957, with the introduction of the third iteration of the Panhead, the Duo-Glide.

The "Duo" in Duo-Glide was Harley's acknowledgment of the most important update to its Big Twin since the Hydra-Glide front end in 1949: a swinging-arm rear suspension with a hydraulically damped shock absorber on each side. For the first time, the rear suspension of Harley's Big Twin was as good as the front.

The rear shocks meant a smoother ride on all roads and a real reduction in the pummeling a rider took on the bumpy ones. The addition of a rear suspension turned a good long-haul bike into a great one. The suspenders fore and aft transformed the Panhead into the undisputed King of the American Road.

That suspension also forced a restyle of the whole rear end that made the old Big Twin seem modern again. As a bonus, the Duo-Glide debuted with hydraulic rear brakes for better stopping power.

Little changed for 1959, but the front end was given a facelift for 1960 that updated the Duo-Glide's looks for the new decade. New aluminum fork shrouds enclosed the headlight in a massive, streamlined unit that proved an essential part of the Big Twin look from the 1960s through the last of the real FLHs, in 1984. Later, Willie G. revived that look with the Road King models.

BELOW AND OPPOSITE, TOP: Tinted windshield lowers were popular during the 1960s. This 1963 FL has a red lower to accent its bright red paint.

ELECTRA GLIDE: THE PUSH-BUTTON PANHEAD

Even as late as the mid-1960s, Harley-Davidson still considered its FLH the company "hot rod." Everyone else knew that Harley's Big Twin had long ago lost the performance war to the smaller Sportster and to British hot rods, such as the Triumph Bonneville and Norton Dominator. Worse yet, Harley's Big Twin began losing yet another skirmish in the 1960s to a new foe.

That skirmish? The push-button wars. The foe? Honda, and soon a slew of other Japanese companies.

In the early 1960s, Harley-Davidson was selling about 10,000 motorcycles a year to hard-core enthusiasts. Upstart Honda, on the other hand, had been in the US market just a few years, yet it was selling bigger and bigger motorcycles by the hundreds of thousands to mainstream Americans.

Sure, there was a huge price difference between Hondas and Harleys, but that didn't really explain the even huger disparity in sales figures. What really distinguished the Honda from the Harley in the eyes of the general public was much simpler: if you wanted to ride your Honda, all you had to do was turn the key and push the start button, but if you wanted to ride your Harley, you had to go through an arcane starting ritual that looked to the uninitiated like equal parts exercise and exorcism. Part of Soichiro Honda's

THE GOOD STUFF WAS HIDDEN FROM VIEW BEHIND NEW COVERS AND CASES, BUT CHROME SCRIPT ON EACH SIDE OF THE FRONT FENDER NAMED HARLEY'S NEW ERA IN A DIALECT ALL FANS WERE SURE TO UNDERSTAND: ELECTRA GLIDE.

By the early 1960s, scofflaws and speeders no longer feared Harley police bikes. Riders on any number of motorcycles could thumb their noses at an officer aboard a Panhead...but they couldn't outrun his radio.

genius was his realization that motorcycles would never appeal to the masses until they were just as easy to start, and as reliable, as a car.

Harley-Davidson caught the push-button vibe for 1965. Outwardly, the 1965 Harley Big Twins looked a little pudgier, but not all that different from the 1964 Duo-Glides. That's because the good stuff was hidden from view behind new covers and cases, but chrome script on each side of the front fender named Harley's new era in a dialect all fans were sure to understand: *Electra Glide*. That's "Electra" as in electric start—and more than anything Harley-Davidson had ever done, this change had a cultural impact.

Kick-starting had always been an honored rite of passage among Big Twin riders. The standard answer to a son's/little brother's/nephew's/neighborhood pest's longing pleas of "When can I ride it?" was "When you learn how to start it." At least that was the answer I got. And it looked like a man-sized job to me at the time. Here's the drill: Choke on one or two clicks. Retard the spark. Open the throttle all the way. Leap up and give a priming kick, and then another. Turn on the ignition. Push slowly down on the kick-starter until you feel the compression build. Gather your strength. Then leap up and come down on the lever with all the force you can muster, while still keeping your demeanor as nonchalant as possible.

The last year for the Panhead—1965—marked the first year for the Electra Glide.

The Electra Glide appealed to a wide variety of riders.

If all is well, the mighty beast springs to life and you feel like a hero.

If not, you kick some more and swear to the gods of the V-twin thunder that you'll give the bike a complete tune-up this Sunday, right after you go to church. And this is not something you want to go through after stalling at an intersection, with a bunch of honking cars behind you.

Die-hard traditionalists were seriously unhappy with the new "Push-Button Pan." Not only had Harley-Davidson taken away their central initiation rite, but the starter and huge new battery added over 75 pounds to an already portly machine. Say hello to the Hog.

Everyone else was thrilled, despite the extra weight, and sales rose by 26 percent. The new E Glide was the biggest-selling Harley Big Twin since 1951, when the British invasion began in earnest.

The Electra Glide was a Harley Big Twin for the motorcycling masses. It was not just for the young and strong. Anyone who could swing a leg over it could start and ride it. Older riders, smaller riders, and those with weak knees could join the sport and cruise America on the ultimate long-haul touring bike of the day.

Unfortunately, it was the last stretch for the venerable Panhead. For 1966, Harley's Overhead Big Twin motor was given yet another top end, and a new era in company history began: The Shovelhead Era.

THE ITALIAN JOB: AERMACCHI H-D

By Greg Field

For a time in the 1920s, Aermacchi was the Air Jordan of seaplane racing, and it built the world's fastest airplanes. Its full name was "Aeronautica Macchi."

Later, Macchi built some very respectable fighters for Mussolini's air force, but those fighters weren't good enough to prevent American flyers from bombing the factory into rubble during World War II. After the war, Aermacchi dusted itself off and began building the small motorcycles that were then the backbone of the Italian transportation system.

When Harley-Davidson wanted to diversify into production of more midsized motorcycles in 1960, Aermacchi seemed a perfect fit, so Harley-Davidson bought 49 percent of the company for a paltry $260,000 (Aermacchi kept 49 percent, and Lockheed owned the "tie-breaking" 2 percent). For 1961, Harley began importing rebadged Aermacchi singles and pushing them on reluctant Harley dealers.

By 1966, Harley was importing more than 20,000 Aermacchi two- and four-strokes a year. Most were two-stroke M50s, and they were sold at fire-sale prices. After that, the four-stroke Sprint caught on and had decent sales and racing success through 1974, when it was canceled.

By then, American Motorcycle Federation owned all of Aermacchi, and AMF directed it to build a series of two-stroke street scramblers and motocrossers, which stacked up in dealerships. Despite that, AMF kept Aermacchi going full-bore. Why?

Vaughn Beals explained: "Italy had this crazy law where you could cut car production, but you couldn't lay off employees. AMF thought, 'We have to pay them, so we might as well have them build bikes.' One day we discovered all these bikes warehoused in Italy, the US, Brazil, and all over that we hadn't sold. Now we couldn't sell them because they hadn't been prepared for storage, so they were all rusted. I finally convinced AMF to shut it down and sell it."

In June 1978, AMF closed the Aermacchi factory. Remnants of Aermacchi live on today, because AMF ultimately sold the factory to the Castiglioni brothers, who build Cagiva and Ducati motorcycles there.

While ultimately proving disastrous for Harley, the Aermacchi connection resulted in some nice motorcycles.

CHAPTER 5

THE SPORTSTER ERA

BY ALLEN GIRDLER

WHAT WE HAVE IN THE SPORTSTER IS A SUCCESS STORY. FROM 1957 THROUGH 2002—FORTY-FIVE YEARS—THE HARLEY-DAVIDSON SPORTSTER HAS WON RACES ON THE TRACK, IN THE SHOWROOM, AND ON THE STREET. THE SPORTSTER HAS ALSO WON THE HEARTS OF HUNDREDS OF THOUSANDS OF OWNERS AND RIDERS.

This success has come despite some flaws, despite some missteps in both engineering and marketing, despite having begun life with genes that originated in 1929, and despite having been introduced to a market that shifted as soon as it was targeted.

Let's begin with those genes. In 1929 Harley-Davidson introduced a line of middleweight twins. In classic H-D form, they featured a 45-degree V angle, but they displaced only 45 cubic inches. They were flatheads, with in-head side valves operated by four one-lobed camshafts arranged in an arc at the engine's lower right, a design used by no Harley or Indian before.

Aside from the side-valve design, the rest of the bike, named the D series, was state of the art for 1929. There were modest changes and revisions, but the basic engine design carried on through 1951.

In 1952, Harley engineers reworked the basic engine. Engine and gearbox were now unit construction, the transmission sported four cogs in the place of three, and a hand clutch and foot shift replaced the foot-clutch hand-shift setup of the old flathead 45. By no coincidence, this arrangement mimicked the setup used by Harley's rivals from England. The new model, the K, had a rear swing arm and shocks, and telescopic forks. This was new technology for Harley-Davidson but standard fare for its rivals.

What the K didn't have was enough power, so in 1954 the engine was given a longer stroke, creating a displacement of 54 cubic inches (or 883cc, so it could be more easily compared with the 650cc English sports bikes).

The larger engine did perform better, especially when it was tuned, but the K, KH, and KHK were better lookers than performers (or sellers).

A new model greeted Harley customers for 1957. The XL Sportster put a whole new take on how Harley-Davidson was going to combat the rising tide of British bikes in America.

THE XL ENGINE HAD THE SAME DISPLACEMENT, 883CC (54 CUBIC INCHES), AS THE KH, BUT IT WASN'T SIMPLY A KH WITH OVERHEAD VALVES.

ENTER THE SPORTSTER

For the 1957 model year, Harley-Davidson introduced the XL Sportster.

The Sportster retained all the modern features—the telescopic forks, swing-arm rear suspension, hand clutch, and foot shift. Brakes were drum, front and rear. The frame was similar to the KH frame but not identical.

The XL engine had the same displacement, 883cc or 54 cubic inches, as the KH, but it wasn't simply a KH with overhead valves. The XL had a larger bore and shorter stroke for better breathing, higher revs, and a higher cruising speed.

The narrow V and the four-cam arc were retained, along with the dry clutch, sealed off (or so they hoped) inside the primary drive cavity, which was filled with lube.

But the XL engine had some odd features. First, the heads and cylinders were cast-iron. Most makers, including Harley with its Panhead, used alloy heads, because they ran cooler and lasted longer. The reason for this has never been explained. Perhaps because the Panheads leaked and gave trouble at first, H-D engineers decided they didn't have the foundry expertise to make aluminum heads and took what they considered a safer path.

The second odd feature was simply odd. With this one exception, all Harley-Davidson engines and families began with one letter, as in J, F, D, W, K, and E. But the Sportster arrived bearing the letters XL.

Historically, the L usually indicated higher compression ratios, as in the EL and DL. Perhaps the model that appeared in 1957 was a higher-compression version of an earlier X prototype. Or perhaps not.

The new Sportster sported a unique tank emblem for 1957. As it turned out, that was the only year for that particular emblem.

The rest of the new model was current. Because this was the day of "Bigger Is Better" in the car world, the original XL arrived looking like a junior FLH, with a large fuel tank, fully balanced fenders, and a large headlight mounted in a nacelle like the one found on the bigger twins. The Sportster was aimed at the guy who wanted a Panhead but couldn't afford the payments.

This wasn't exactly wrong, and the new XL sold well. It was attractive and much faster than the KH, even though the claimed horsepower rating had only gone from 38 to 40.

Although Harley continued to race its side-valve KR models rather than the XL-based overhead-valve machines, the company's engineers developed some overhead-valve racers based on the XL. They combined the KR's ball bearing lower end, magneto ignition, and open pipes with the XL's cylinders and an improved version of the XL's heads, with larger valves and higher compression ratio. They added a racing carburetor and hotter camshaft timing.

The model was named XLR, which was logical, and it was introduced for the 1958 model year.

Meanwhile, when the California dealers saw the new XL, they were impressed with its potential. They told the national guys that fans riding in the woods and deserts back home in the West needed and deserved something better than the Hummers and 165s Harley-Davidson offered.

To provide these dealers with a competitive motorcycle, Harley took the peanut tank, open pipes, and skimpy fenders from the XLR and installed a nearly stock XL engine, minus generator and lights but with the KR magneto.

The 1957 Sportster was lean and trim, but it had yet to attain the identity that makes it stand out today. That identity feature, of course, is the peanut gas tank.

ABOVE: Like the British bikes it was designed to compete against, the new Sportster had right-side shifting, with the rear brake pedal on the left side.

RIGHT: The Sportster's standard exhaust system routed its two header pipes into a single muffler.

This model was named XLC. California dealers Armando Magri and Len Andres said the letter C was for their state, but it most likely stood for "Competition."

The XLC didn't appear in the history books for years. Harley only sold a handful during the two years it was in the catalog. The XLR barely got a mention. Perhaps a few hundred were built and sold during the years the model was offered for sale (1958–1969). Still, both models proved influential. The motorcycle world of the later 1950s was kind of like a small town. People knew what other people were up to, and word of the XLC and XLR got out.

New colors and a new gas tank emblem were among the offerings for customers of 1958 Sportsters.

ENTER THE SUPERBIKE

Harley engineers had learned that the 9:1 compression ratio of the XLR was safe in street use, with the normal gasoline of the day, so for 1958 they introduced a higher-compression H version of the XL.

For the ultimate XL model, Harley engineers combined or expanded the best features of the XLC, XLR, and XLH, creating a machine with the normal street-livable lower end of the XL, the tuning of the XLH, and the bare bones appeal of the XLC. There was the little tank, open pipes, skimpy fenders, and magneto ignition, but the engine on the new model used a rollers-and-bushings lower end that would run for years.

Its name was XLCH.

No motorcycle ever looked better than this minimal machine, with its classic, muscular profile.

That first year, 1958, the XLCH came stripped, and with the low, separate open pipes of the KR and XLR. All the dealers knew their customers and reported to the factory, so for 1959 the XLCH game came as a road bike, with lights, generator, and points-and-coil timer atop the gear case.

ABOVE: Unlike the standard XL version, the 1958 XLCH was created for on-track performance. Light weight, hotter camshafts, and two open exhaust pipes were among its features.

RIGHT: The XLCH was devoid of lights and other features not necessary for racing. The rear fender was also bobbed to reduce weight.

The factory fitted the XLCH with a Siamese exhaust system. The stock muffler didn't muffle much, so sound and performance were fine. Even so, the first thing the XLCH buyer did was remove the Siamese pipe and fit a pair of low shorty duals, as seen on the KR, because that was what looked cool. Today, a stock high exhaust is a Sportster restorer's dream find.

The big nacelle and headlight on the XL were too large for the rest of the XLCH, so someone came up with an eyebrow mount for the smaller headlight. (The eyebrow mount is still with us, on both the XL and FX model lines.) The XLCH ruled. The CH was sparse and tuned to a point where it would outperform anything in the English stable, and even the sporting Japanese machines. It simply destroyed any car on the road. While not the absolutely most powerful or the fastest motorcycle a person could buy, the XLCH was the highest-performance motorcycle anyone could find at a nearby store. And everyone knew it.

The CH could be temperamental. A magneto produces more power with more rpm, which means less power at lower speeds, making kick-starting a challenge. Spark timing was manually adjusted, which meant if the rider forgot, he was reminded by a literal kick in the shins. Or the sometimes-weak spring wouldn't engage the ratchet, and he'd kick against no resistance, which also hurt. And the XLCH required a lot of kicks, especially after the adoption in 1966 of a radical new carburetor, which worked fine once the tricks had been deciphered.

Nor was daily operation trouble free. The clutch was supposed to run dry, allowing relatively soft springs for ease of operation. But the seals leaked. The oil pump's drive pin was known to shear; the ignition timing gear could slip on its shaft; the right rear case half was weak. All of these traits established the XLCH rider as a man of skill and determination, a motorcyclist who paid his dues.

Early XLCHs weighed 480 or 490 pounds, but in 1967 the XLH, with a larger fuel tank and electric start, weighed 510 pounds. All versions of the XLCH would cover the standing-start quarter-mile in less than 15 seconds and would top 110 miles per hour with an occasional burst up to 120, and they returned 40 to 60 miles per gallon and about 250 to 500 miles per quart of oil.

GENTLER, KINDER . . . AND BIGGER

By the late 1960s, the superbike market segment was larger—and faster. Triumph and BSA came out with 750cc four-stroke triples. Kawasaki's ferocious two-stroke triples were even faster and scarier than the British four-strokes, and in 1970, Honda introduced the 750cc four.

Harley-Davidson took a different tack. In 1970, the XLCH got a coil-and-points ignition, which made it easier to start. That year an optional fiberglass seat/fender was used for the 1971 Superglide, in spite of the fact that nobody ordered one for a Sportster. In 1971, the ignition timer was replaced by points inside a housing on the gear case cover, and the dry clutch was replaced by a wet clutch—harder on the hand but easier on maintenance. Boring the cylinders to 3.188 inches gave the 1972 XL more displacement, increasing capacity to 61 cubic inches, though the larger XL engine was called a 1,000, probably because the competition used metric measurements.

By this time Harley-Davidson was a division of AMF (American Machine & Foundry), and because the XL line was outselling the FL line, AMF allowed annual improvements but no major changes. Many of the model year variations were matters of style. The CH's peanut tank was standard for both models, and the standard seat was a skimpy plank, replacing the thicker and softer dual saddle. Comfort went down, but sales went up.

THE CH COULD BE TEMPERAMENTAL. A MAGNETO PRODUCES MORE POWER WITH MORE RPM, WHICH MEANS LESS POWER AT LOWER SPEEDS, MAKING KICK-STARTING A CHALLENGE.

The 1958 XLCH proved so successful that Harley-Davidson added lights and other equipment to make it street legal for 1959.

The front brake was converted to disc in 1973, and in 1974, thanks to the federal mandate, the throttle got a return spring. That same year, the feds dictated that motorcycle shift levers were to be located on the left side rather than the right. Since the XL gearbox had been designed to mimic its English rivals, the shift shaft emerged on the right side of the cases. Harley used a system of linkages to move the shift lever from right to left. In 1976, Harley revised the cases and gearbox so the shift shaft emerged on the left.

In a clear case of good intentions, the 1976 line included another model, the XLT, a touring bike. It had the lovely 3.5-gallon teardrop fuel tank first seen on the Italian sprints, rather than the 2.25-gallon peanut tank, and the dual seat was thicker. Final drive was geared higher for a relaxed highway gait. It didn't sell, and the XLT was dropped after two model years. As Samuel Goldwyn said, "If people don't want to go to the movies, you can't stop them."

Late in the 1977 model year came something really different. This XL frame was derived from the KH frame. This wasn't as stiff as it could have been, but the frame was good enough for 1950s-era tire and suspension technology. When tires and suspensions improved, and the addition of the electric starter and larger battery added weight and moved things around, the space between the shocks and engine were so cramped that on occasion the chain would saw through the corner of the oil tank.

When the Racing and Engineering Departments were working on the XR-750 racer, they drew up a vastly better frame. It was stiffer and more predictable, and there was room behind the engine.

THE XLCR

While the XR-750 project was underway, William G. Davidson, third-generation member of the founding family and Harley's head of styling, believed the company needed additional models and more press coverage, and it needed to achieve both on a tight budget.

The XLCR project began with a redesigned XR frame.

Into this frame went a blacked-out XL engine. The bodywork was vaguely based on the XR-750, with solo seat and a tapering tail, low bars, rear set pegs, and a bikini fairing. A bit before this time, the English bike nuts had begun modifying sports models to mimic road racers, with low bars, rear set controls, and souped-up engines. They used the machines on the street, racing from hangout to hangout, and the bikes were known as café racers. Willie G. knew of this trend, and because some elements of the modified XL were in that vein, the new model was named XLCR. The XLCR came with a better seat than did the normal XLH. The gearing was lower so the dragstrip times were better. As the XLCR came from the factory, it was a good machine, an improvement in important ways. But after it left the factory, it didn't sell. In the long run, the XLCR became a collector's bike and has held its value much better than other models in its class, but at the same time, the model was a commercial failure.

Model year 1979 marked the last year for the XLCH, which really hadn't been a distinct model since the loss of the magneto and the acquisition of electric start. In its place came the XLS, another attempt to make a new model from existing parts. The name of the new XLS was Roadster, chosen via a nationwide contest. Featuring drag bars on risers and mildly extended forks, the roadster was marketed as a Sportster version of the popular FX Low Rider.

The high-mounted two-into-one exhaust system was unique to the XLCH for 1959.

ABOVE: By 1964, two Sportster variations were offered, the XLH and the XLCH. The front die-cast aluminum brake improved stopping power.

RIGHT: Electric starting found its way into the Sportster lineup for 1967. This XLH also has a dual-passenger white seat, giving the bike a rather subdued appearance by Sportster standards.

TWO MOVES, OPPOSITE DIRECTIONS

AMF invested a ton of money in H-D's plants, and into planning for improved products, but AMF executives weren't good with people. Some bad feelings remain among Harley fans and former employees over the unrest and labor troubles from the AMF years. But, the improved infrastructure and the money for research and development gave Harley a base from which to launch better motorcycles, which it did.

After a group of investors bought Harley-Davidson from AMF, the first thing the new owners did to the Sportster family was introduce what's known in the retail world as a loss leader.

For 1983, Harley introduced a stripped Sportster model with a peanut tank, solo seat, and low bars. It came only in black and had hardly any chrome, even on the exhaust pipes. Harley named its new Sportster the XLX-61—none of this metric foolishness—and the suggested retail price was $3,995, marginally less expensive than an optioned XLH and much less expensive than a Harley Big Twin. The price was right in the neighborhood of comparable imports. The model run sold out. Fast.

To create another Sportster-based model, H-D's Racing Department took two-carb aluminum alloy XR-750 cylinder heads, made special alloy cylinders, and adapted the top end to a modified version of the XL cases. They mounted two carburetors on the right and two exhaust pipes on the left, just like an XR-750.

Representing a raw, visceral look, this 1968 XLCH was among the fastest and quickest motorcycles offered at the time.

They put the mix-and-match engine in an XLX frame and tagged the model the XR-1000.

Actually, it was a bit more complicated than that. The XL and XR engines had diverged in major ways since their common ancestry began, and the actual XR heads wouldn't fit on the XL cases, while the XR heads were too tall for the XL frame.

The new model needed new cases and a whole lot more, most of which wasn't readily apparent to the naked eye. Thus, when the XR-1000 appeared as a 1983 model, it was priced at $7,000—nearly twice the asking price for the XLX—when it only had 10 or so more horsepower than the stock XL-1000 engine. And while the tests showed the XR-1000 to be the quickest Harley ever, it wasn't close to the times turned by the 750cc fours in the rival showrooms. Worse yet, the Engineering Department had done the work too quickly. There were serious flaws in the XR-1000's basic design: they broke early and often.

What might have been the true third strike against the XR-1000 was that it didn't look all that different from the XLX or an XHL. It featured no bodywork, no streamlining, no road-going fairing, nor anything besides those two carburetors sticking out on the right side to indicate it was anything more than a pedestrian XLX.

The XR-1000, like the XLCR, didn't sell and was dropped from the lineup after two years.

But the XR-1000 wasn't a total disaster. The XLX may have sold hot dogs at halftime, but the profit margin was terribly thin. The XR-1000 sold like sand in the desert, but because of its big markup, the XR-1000 actually put some money in the bank when the banks were about to call in the loans. And like other models the public didn't want, the XR-1000 is now a collector's item—so valuable that owners show them rather than ride them.

The staggered mufflers with bullet tips highlighted XLH styling for 1970. There also was a new ignition system for the year.

ABOVE: The optional boat-tail rear-seat section that was optional for 1970 returned to the Sportster lineup for 1971 too. It was a styling trend that never caught on.

LEFT: Optional weatherproof hard saddlebags and a full-length windshield help make this 1970 XLH more roadworthy for travel.

The XLCR helped usher in the Sportster's new frame, dual-front disc brakes, and a Siamese exhaust system.

COMES THE EVOLUTION

From the company's beginning, it's been an H-D policy to make improvements one or two at a time. For the 1986 model year, the Sportster got a new Evolution engine. In something of a break with Harley tradition, just about everything about the Evo engine was new.

The profile and the general outline were the same, but the new engine's cylinders and heads were aluminum alloy, and because they would let the engine run cooler under load, they could be more heavily stressed to produce more power. A few weeks after debuting the XLH-883, the factory introduced the XLH-1100 Sportster. The 1100, created by increasing the cylinder bore, was quicker than the old Ironhead XL-1000 and as quick as rival 1,000cc twins from across either ocean.

Priced at $3,995 for a stripped model with solo seat and black paint, the Evo-powered XL-883 was a bargain. The 1100 didn't come in a stripped version. Besides, the 1100 still sold for $2,000 less than the least expensive Big Twin.

THE HUGGER'S SECRET

Women have been riding motorcycles since the motorcycle was invented, but it wasn't until the 1980s that manufacturers began to recognize this fact. Harley-Davidson also recognized some basic physical differences between men and women, most notably that women usually aren't as tall as men. Beginning with the 1980 model year, Harley offered an XLH with shorter rear shock absorbers, the fork tubes slippered up in their clamps, and less padding in the seat. These minor changes resulted in the lowest static seat height on the market. The new model was named Hugger, and it was just like any other XLH except for the suspension and the seat. The Hugger has been a strong seller since it was introduced, and a sizeable portion of that market segment is female.

THE 1200

The 1,100cc Sportster had performed well and proven reliable, so for 1988, the bore was increased again, raising the displacement to 1,200.

This time, though, there was more involved than a larger bore. The 1200 used larger valves and ports, along with a larger combustion chamber.

One of the most iconic Sportsters ever is the 1977 XLCR that boasted café styling as perceived by Willie G. Davidson.

FIVE SPEEDS . . . AND MORE

The 1991 XLH got two major improvements.

First, the engineers figured how to put five pairs of gears where four had been since the first model K appeared in 1952. When the engineers were packing the fifth set of gears inside the cavity, they revised and improved the shift drum and linkage, so the 1991 and subsequent XLs are much easier to shift, with lighter controls and fewer grinding noises.

The second major modification was a switch to belt drive, long a feature of the Big Twins. The belt drive first arrived on the 1,200cc Sportster. This proved so popular that for the 1993 model year all the XLs came stock with belt drive, which is much cleaner, needs virtually no maintenance, and lasts two or three times as long as the best chain ever did.

The next few years saw mostly minor changes, such as larger fuel tanks, until the introduction of the Custom and Sport versions of the 1,200cc model in 1996. The Custom came with raised handlebars, a stepped seat, and a 21-inch front wheel. It sold well. The Sport had stickier tires, low bars, and tunable suspension, and didn't sell as well.

The big Sportster news for 1999 was the introduction of an 883cc version of the Custom. For 2002, Harley introduced the XL-883R, a racy-looking Sportster with a stock two-into-one exhaust and big muffler, a streamlined seat and low bars, and, perhaps best of all, the darker orange paint seen on the VR-1000 and XR-750 factory racers.

THE UNBROKEN CIRCLE

The more things change, the more they remain the same.

When the Sportster appeared in 1957, it arrived as an air-cooled, narrow-angle, V-twin with modern suspension, brakes, and controls, and with a profile that somehow combined the traditional and the radical. As the Sportster appeared again on the eve of

The mid-1970s Sportsters are valued for their classic lines. This 1975 XLH shows off its tight-fitting banana seat.

TOP: The 75th Anniversary Edition XLH wore the same front brakes as seen on the XLCR, and its balony-cut muffler represented a styling trend of the time.

BOTTOM LEFT: Harley-Davidson's 75th anniversary celebration in 1978 included a special Anniversary Edition XLH that was anchored by its black paint with gold striping.

BOTTOM RIGHT: The XR1000 was Harley's bad boy on the block in 1984. Its 1,000cc engine breathed through two Mikuni carburetors that ultimately fed two hot-rod-style exhausts.

ABOVE: A new Evolution-based Sportster engine showed up in 1986, first as an 883cc version that was joined by a 1,200cc model. This is a 1998 XL1200C.

RIGHT: Unique gas tank graphics earmark the 1986 XLH1100. The iconic peanut gas tank became a staple with Evo Sportsters.

Harley's XR750 flat-track racer is based on early Sportster designs. Conversely, this 2002 XL883R takes its styling cues from the XR750.

Harley-Davidson's second century of building motorcycles in 2002, it was an air-cooled, narrow-angle, overhead-valve V-twin with modern suspension, brakes, and controls, and with a profile that still combined the traditional and the radical.

But in the intervening years, all the details changed. The Sportster's lifespan was a time of major technical improvement. The 2002 Sportster was an incomparably better motorcycle than the 1957 XL was, never mind what Granddad says.

Which brings us, if not quite to the future, to at least wondering what the Sportster's future will be. The Sportster is limited, if not quite imprisoned, by the success of the model line and the parent company. When the grandparent D series 45s arrived in 1929, they were an answer to rival Indian's middleweight Scouts.

When the water-cooled V-Rod arrived in 2001, it was an answer to the rival big-engine sports cruisers from overseas. In an H-D dealership near you, there's the single-cylinder Buell Blast, and the Buell Twins to compete against the sporting twins from east and west. The Softails and Dyna Glides take the factory chopper further than the XL Customs will ever dare to go.

Not long before the V-Rod was introduced, H-D's chief engineer made a point of stressing the company's commitment to air cooling. "Never mind the federal mandates for emissions and noise," he said. "We can meet those requirements, and we'll never surrender the simplicity and reliability of using the air stream for cooling."

What this means, at this time and in this context, is that the Sportster doesn't have many directions in which it can go. If the models got much smaller or much larger, they'd compete with other Harleys. If Sportsters had four cylinders or radiators, they wouldn't be Sportsters.

What we can expect is continued improvement, evolution if you will, with perhaps a version of the Buell's isolation engine mounts to tame the vibration that remains the XL's only true drawback.

Beyond that, as long as the Sportster sells, the Sportster will be produced. If the Sportster ain't broke, don't fix it.

THE BIG NACELLE AND HEADLIGHT ON THE XL WERE TOO LARGE FOR THE REST OF THE XLCH, SO SOMEONE CAME UP WITH AN EYEBROW MOUND FOR THE SMALLER HEADLIGHT.

CHAPTER 6

THE SHOVELHEAD ERA

BY GREG FIELD

FOR MOST OF ITS FIRST CENTURY, THE MOTORCYCLES HARLEY-DAVIDSON BUILT DEFINED THE COMPANY, BUT THAT WAS NOT THE CASE BETWEEN 1966 AND 1984. THE DRAMA THAT PLAYED OUT WITHIN THE MOTOR COMPANY DURING THE SHOVELHEAD ERA OVERSHADOWED THE MOTORCYCLES IT BUILT. THAT'S NOT TO SAY HARLEY-DAVIDSON DIDN'T BUILD SOME GREAT MOTORCYCLES DURING THE ERA, BECAUSE IT PRODUCED SOME VERY IMPORTANT MODELS. BUT AS IMPORTANT AS THOSE MODELS WERE, THEY PALED NEXT TO THE IMPORTANCE OF THE BATTLES THAT RAGED AT THE VERY TOP OF HARLEY-DAVIDSON'S CORPORATE HIERARCHY.

This was a time when the clannish family owners first sold shares to the public, before the clan splintered and put the whole company on the auction block. It was the era when Harley's board of directors fought off a corporate vampire bent on sucking the company dry and found a white knight to take over under favorable terms. In time, that white knight started looking more like the wicked witch, as it expanded production beyond all imagining, clashed mightily with its workforce, ripped the company in two, and shredded its good reputation. Most importantly, it was the era when a core group of heroes bought back the Motor Company after everyone had written it off for dead, then took the company to undreamed-of heights.

It was the Shovelhead era. Like all eras worth looking at, it began long before the history books say it did, so let's rewind to the real beginning.

IT WAS A CLAN THING

By beginning, we really mean beginning, as in 1903 through 1907. Bill Harley and the Davidson brothers were tight, but the Davidsons ran everything while Harley was off earning an engineering degree.

The Davidson boys were sons of Scottish immigrants, so *clan* was not just a word. They had been raised on the principle that if you need help, you turn to your clan, which in this case was the extended Davidson family in and around Milwaukee.

When they needed more space, Dad built a shed for them. When they were hungry, Mom cooked for them. When they needed someone to paint the company name on the building or on the new machines, a sister did it. When they needed someone to keep the books, another sister pitched in. When they needed a loan, they turned to a bachelor uncle. Though they didn't go so far as to paint their first bikes tartan plaid, the Davidsons were Scots to a fault.

When Harley-Davidson incorporated in 1907, its board of directors became the clan chieftains. The clan grew as the families grew, and all management positions were filled from sons of chieftains. In turn, the chieftains managed the company to maximize profits back to the clan. The clan's first loyalty was to the company, and the company's first loyalty was to the clan.

That clan stayed tight and grew rich through the gravy years of the 1910s and 1920s. During the tough years of the 1930s, the growth years of the 1940s, and the British invasion of the 1950s, this clannishness served the company well. "If a problem came up, they could just get the family together in a room and solve it," explained Vaughn Beals, the man who would later lead Harley back to glory.

By the early 1960s, however, the clannishness wasn't working so well. Clan loyalty to the company had been diluted over three generations, the new clan chieftains weren't necessarily the best men for the job, and clannish emphasis on paying shareholders before investing in new equipment and designs had left Harley with outdated factories and designs—just as the Japanese moved in.

It could be said that Harley's clannishness had turned a proud, kilted Highland piper into the toothless, inbred banjo picker of the motorcycle industry.

WHAT WE HAVE HERE IS A FAILURE TO DIVERSIFY

Most of the Harley and Davidson clans neither worked for the company, nor cared about the motorcycles. The predominant attitude was: "My entire fortune is tied up in some stupid motorcycle company founded by my father (or grandfather or husband's father), and I think I could make more money if that money was invested in Coca-Cola or McDonald's."

These later generations had also grown financially savvy. They knew it was risky to have all their financial eggs in one basket. What they and Harley-Davidson needed was to diversify. Harley's first steps toward diversification came in 1960, when it began building scooters and bought into the Italian firm Aermacchi to get a new line of lightweight motorcycles. In 1962, Harley bought the Tomahawk boat works and began building golf carts and boats.

Further diversification and upgrades to the plants required capital that neither the company nor the stockholders had. And the stockholders couldn't diversify for themselves because no one else in the clan had the money to buy their stock. That put clan chieftains Gordon, Walter, and William H. Davidson and William J. Harley in a real bind. Their

HARLEY SENT FEELERS OUT IN ITS SEARCH FOR A BUYER, AND THE MAJOR COMPANIES THAT RESPONDED INCLUDED CATERPILLAR, JOHN DEERE, OMC, AND CHRIS-CRAFT.

The year after the electric starter found its way onto the Panhead engine, Harley came back with an updated FL that earned the moniker "Shovelhead."

own fortunes were tied up too, and the folks breathing down their necks were kin, not anonymous investors. And if they didn't find some money soon, clan and company would probably wither and die together.

GOING PUBLIC

The only way out was to break with clan tradition and sell stock to the general public for the first time. Harley's directors split the stock two-for-one and made a first offering of 75,000 shares for the company and about 24,000 from its shareholders, which all quickly sold. Harley-Davidson spent its share on plant expansions in Italy, Milwaukee, and at Tomahawk, boosting its workforce by 20 percent.

Despite the infusion of cash, money was still very tight, according to Tom Gelb, then plant superintendent and later one of the saviors of the company. "They let me buy one machine tool a year. Nobody believes this now, but we still used box wrenches on the production line because there was no money for pneumatic tools. I had a feeling the company wasn't going to last, so I left," he said.

THE FIRST SHOVELHEAD

That brings us to the namesake of this era, created when Harley updated the Panhead engine for 1966. Like the Panhead before it, the new engine wasn't all that new. Mostly, it was a new top end on the old Panhead bottom end. Its marquee feature was a set of U-shaped rocker boxes that enclosed the valve gear but left more head area exposed for better cooling. Squinted at from the bike's right side, after a few too many beers, the cover's shape resembled the back of a coal shovel, earning the nickname "Shovelhead."

With the investment brought in by the stock sale and the sales bump brought on by the new engine, 1966 was the most successful year in company history. Sales rose to 36,310, the most the company had ever sold in one year. True, many of these were the lightweights built by Aermacchi, but revenue and profits were the best they'd ever been.

For 1967, Harley once again gave the Electra Glide a few updates. Sales were down a bit compared to 1966, but profits were up because the expensive Electra Glides and Sportsters sold as well as before. Little was changed for 1968, but sales remained steady, leading to record revenue and great profit margins.

An outside observer could easily think all was well in Harleyland. Unfortunately, all was far from well.

BREAKING UP THE CLAN

Despite diversification and good profits, the stockholders wanted more. Problem was, there was no longer a quick way to raise the money to diversify. After the last issuance of "print-and-sell" stock, members of the clan only owned 53 percent of outstanding shares. If they sold stock or the company printed more, the clan would lose its majority control.

This crisis split the clan into two camps. "We could diversify two ways," explained John Davidson, board member and son of then-president William H. Davidson. "We could start building lawn mowers and so on, or we could get sucked up. The merger group held the majority and won, so we began looking for someone to buy the company."

SEARCHING FOR A SUGAR DADDY

Harley quietly sent feelers out in its search for a buyer, and the major companies that responded included Caterpillar, John Deere, OMC, and Chris-Craft. One by one, these potential buyers backed out, some after seeing the sorry state of the company's plants and processes, others after personality conflicts with the clan. In one case, the suitor decided it didn't want to be associated with the "criminal" element attracted to Harleys. Some say all the deals were sabotaged by President William H. Davidson, who didn't want to sell at all.

ALL HELL BREAKS LOOSE

One impatient Harley stockholder finally forced William H.'s hand. Through a broker, that stockholder approached the rapidly growing conglomerate of Bangor Punta (BP), and soon, all hell broke loose.

On May 24, 1968, BP quietly approached Harley's board with an offer to buy H-D for $27 per share. It was a pretty good offer, because H-D stock typically traded for $14 to $20 at the time.

Suddenly, it was high-pucker time in the Harley boardroom. BP had been in the news lately because it was just then acquiring another Milwaukee institution, Waukesha Motors. And BP was widely viewed as a corporate Count Dracula that moved in quickly to suck a company dry whenever it smelled blood. Harley would need to find a white knight to beat back the vampire.

CORPORATE VAMPIRE?

The characterization of BP as a corporate vampire may or may not be fair. BP was a highly diversified company, the result of a *ménage à trios* between potatoes, sugar, and

AS SOON AS THE MERGER PAPERS WERE SIGNED, AMF BEGAN PUMPING MONEY INTO MILWAUKEE, ALLOWING HARLEY TO UPDATE FACILITIES, REDESIGN THE XR-750 TO MAKE IT A WINNER, AND TO IMPROVE THE BIG TWINS AND SPORTSTERS.

Perhaps the most significant change to the
FL for 1967 included the Tillotson carburetor.
Owners either loved or hated the carb. There
was no in between.

railroading. It was formed when the Bangor & Aroostook Railroad merged with the Punta Alegre Sugar Corp.

Vampire or not, BP was an unstoppable acquisition machine that was virtually sheltered from taxation after Castro had seized the company's Cuban sugar factories, giving it a $54 million "paper" loss that the company used to great advantage. By 1968, companies it controlled built products as varied as guns (Smith & Wesson), chemical mace, breathalyzers, motor homes, boats, and industrial machinery. Most of these companies are still around, so it's doubtful that BP's reputation matched reality.

That doesn't matter, though, because William H. Davidson and the board believed that reputation. As the last dyed-in-the-plaid remnants of the clan, they loved both the company and their jobs, so they unanimously rejected BP's offer and intensified their search for other suitors.

Spurned in its friendly takeover attempt, BP bared its fangs on October 1, and took its offer directly to the shareholders. This time the offer was upped to about $32 per share, nearly 50 percent above market.

Harley fought back, calling the offer "inadequate" and emphasizing that the exchange was taxable. Despite that, BP was able to buy or get options on 16.3 percent of the Harley stock, most from builder Chris-Craft, which had earlier looked at buying H-D.

WHITE KNIGHT?

Harley-Davidson found its white knight in American Machine & Foundry, better known as AMF, and announced on October 31 that it had already struck a deal for a tax-free exchange on 1.23 shares of AMF (worth about $29) for each share of H-D stock.

Like Harley-Davidson, AMF was a turn-of-the-century company, and like BP, it was hell-bent on diversification. "AMF was the result of an antitrust action in the early part of the century, in which the tobacco makers were forced to divest themselves of manufacturing the machinery that processed tobacco and made cigarettes," explained Vaughn Beals. "They then began acquiring leisure businesses." Those businesses included boats (Hatteras) and bowling pin setters.

What set AMF apart was its chairman, Rodney Gott, who in his pitch emphasized that he was a longtime Harley fan and offered advice on fending off BP's hostile takeover. "Rodney Gott was a great pitchman," remembered John Davidson. "He sold us a real bill of goods, telling us he would keep Harley-Davidson's management in place and that we would be autonomous."

BIDDING WAR

A big formality remained, however. Under Wisconsin law, a proposed merger took effect only if at least two-thirds of a company's shares approved. BP's goal became to get one third of the shares so it could stop the AMF merger. Accordingly, it offered $40 a share.

That started a comical bidding war between BP and AMF that resulted in a doubling of company value. (BP's final offer was $49 per share, tax-free; AMF's was 1.5 shares, worth about $40 per share, again tax-free.) Though BP's offer was by far the best, Harley's board stuck with AMF and drove a stake through the vampire's heart by calling a shareholder's meeting for December 18, 1968, to vote on the AMF merger.

Undeterred, BP rose again to file suit against Harley for $7 million, the amount BP claimed shareholders were losing by accepting AMF's offer.

Police departments continued using Harleys, and this 1970 FLP is outfitted with some of the basic equipment available to all agencies.

THE FATEFUL VOTE

When William H. Davidson called the shareholder's meeting to order on December 18, BP's president, David W. Wallace, was allowed to speak first. He showed his chutzpah by making one last offer: BP would drop the lawsuit if AMF would raise its offer to two full shares for each one of Harley's. That motion was rejected, the polls opened and closed, and the meeting was adjourned, all inside twenty minutes.

When the results were announced later that afternoon, 78 percent had voted to merge, even though AMF's offer was 20 percent less than BP's.

All that stood between Harley-Davidson and the merger was a vote of the AMF stockholders, a formality scheduled for January 7, 1969, in New York. Inside members of the clan advised each other to sell quickly. Could they have known what AMF had planned?

PAPER EXCHANGE

On January 7, AMF's stockholders met at Carnegie Hall and approved the merger. The next day, the Harley-Davidson Motor Company, Inc. became AMF Harley-Davidson. Based on the prices that day, AMF paid $38.80 per share, or $27,685,895 total.

But that's on paper.

At the same meeting, AMF's board approved the issue of 20 million new shares of AMF stock. All they needed was just more than 1 million to cover the buyout of H-D, leaving enough new stock to cover about 18 similar-sized buyouts in the future or to invest in the business.

AMF's actual cost for Harley-Davidson was the expenses to negotiate and consummate the deal and print some stock. AMF's shareholders paid, though, especially the new ones from Harley-Davidson, through dilution of equity. Those members of the H-D clan who sold out right away did OK, but those who didn't saw their fortune decline with AMF's.

THE HONEYMOON

Like most marriages, that between AMF and Harley began well. As soon as the merger papers were signed, AMF began pumping money into Milwaukee, allowing Harley to update facilities, redesign the XR-750 to make it a winner, and to improve the Big Twins and Sportsters.

At first, anyway, AMF even seemed to follow through on the promise to let Harley run itself.

THE "CONE SHOVEL"

The first and most obvious update came for 1970, when the Shovelhead engine was revised to replace its external generator with an alternator inside the primary case, and to replace the external ignition timer with an automatic-advance ignition inside a new cone-shaped cover on the right of the engine. That cone-shaped cover inspired a new nickname: "Cone Shovelhead."

Other than the cone, little changed on the Electra Glide. It was still an old man's bike amid the greatest youth market the world had ever known.

SUPER GLIDE: "THANK GOD FOR THOSE CHOPPER GUYS!"

Nineteen seventy-one was a huge year for Harley. It was the year the glaciers thawed, the guard changed, production exploded, a new star rose, and a new legend began.

Before 1971, Harley's attitudes were seemingly still stuck in the 1930s and 1940s. To Harley, the words *motorcycle club* still meant AMA clubs riding in formation with their squeaky-clean matching uniforms, and the word *motorcycle* meant a decked-out Big Twin.

Harley's managers knew that the growing clubs were the so-called "outlaws," and those who aped the fashion. And they knew these guys loved stripped and chopped Harleys. Harley could have cashed in on the movement from the start, but president William H. Davidson and the others went far out of their way to avoid any association with the chopper boys.

Harley-Davidson accessory catalogs of the day prove how out of touch the company was. Want "bologna-slicer" bumpers, extra lights, or saddlebags? "We've got every color and style in stock." Want a tall sissy bar or a skinny front wheel (let alone a 10-inch over fork)? "Get the hell out of my dealership, kid!"

Bad as that was for the H-D's bottom line, the real problem the chopper movement presented was that these guys intended to strip off so much of the FLH anyway that they saw no need to buy new, getting by quite nicely with the cast-off Knuckleheads and Panheads of yesteryear.

UNSOLD BIKES BEGAN STACKING UP IN DEALERSHIPS ACROSS THE COUNTRY, SO HARLEY FILED SUIT IN APRIL 1978 AGAINST THE JAPANESE MAKERS, CLAIMING THEY WERE DUMPING EXCESS PRODUCT IN AMERICA.

Fortunately, at least one person at Juneau Avenue was watching—Willie G. Davidson. He'd been watching for a while too, first when he was in design school in California, and later at events he attended after joining the Motor Company in 1963. Even more fortunate: he held the keys to the Styling Department.

For 1971, he gave the chopper guys what they wanted: the FX-1200 Super Glide. There was Willie G.™ (Yes, Harley even has a trademark on his name; the "G" is for "Godfrey") was, innocently wheeling a Sportster front end down to the styling studio, when he turned a corner and, Bam! He ran smack into another guy wheeling a forkless FLH the other way. Instant karma again. So he took it all back to "Willie World" (not yet trademarked) and started bolting it together.

Front end and chassis looked great together, so he played with the rest. Clunky bits, like the footboards, starter, big battery, and fat rear fender were banished to the scrap bin. Same with the exhaust, replaced by a two-into-one that fit the theme. The tanks seemed a bit fat, so he fitted the smaller 3.5-gallon versions. For the final custom touch, he bolted on the optional boattail seat fender from the Sportster. Then, he painted it all up in red, white, and blue as a nod to both patriotism and the Captain America chopper from *Easy Rider*.

It was the first factory "custom" and the boldest, most original styling statement from Harley-Davidson since the 1936 Knucklehead. It wasn't quite a masterpiece, mostly because of the boattail, which most people quickly replaced with a regular Sportster rear fender, but it was the start of a whole new line and whole new legend for the Motor Company.

It melted the glacier between the chopper guys and the Motor Company forever. Suddenly, Harley had a new bike the chopper crowd wanted, and Harley dealers had a compelling reason to invite them in. "Thank God for these chopper guys," said John Davidson, then executive vice president in charge of marketing. "They're the most loyal customers in the world, and they kept the company alive for a lot of years."

It was also the debut of a new star for Harley. The Super Glide announced Willie G.'s arrival. Tom Gelb remembered, "In later years, Willie G. was given a lot of credit for things that Louie Netz [Willie's right-hand man in styling] actually did, but the Super Glide was his baby."

Reportedly, Willie had refined the concept and had it all ready to go by about 1967, but H-D management still despised the chopper crowd too much to ever build a bike for them, and also they thought the new model would only take away from the Sportster sales. Thus, it didn't come to market until 1971, when AMF twisted the throttle.

CHANGING OF THE GUARD

And AMF truly was in control by late 1971.

Rodney Gott's pitch about autonomy for Harley-Davidson turned out to be "a lot of B.S.," according to John Davidson.

President William H. Davidson was "promoted" to chairman of the board, but it was really just a ceremonial position, because there was really no board. "They told William H., 'Go travel the world. Do whatever you want, but get out of our hair,'" explained John Davidson.

In William H.'s place, AMF installed John O'Brien as president, and he ramped up production and brought in battalions of AMF experts. "Every day an expert on something would show up at our door," said John Davidson. "They thought they could do everything better."

The change in the balance of power was plain for all to see when the 1972 models were released: "AMF" had pride of place preceding "Harley-Davidson" on the new tank badges. Balancing that out was the change to hydraulic disc front brakes, which everyone lauded as a huge improvement over the old drum brakes.

HARLEY OR HONDA?

Before long, AMF and O'Brien revealed their real plan: "They actually thought they could turn us into another Honda," guffawed John Davidson. AMF screwed the factory's throttle full on and tried to catch Honda.

That caused immense problems in Milwaukee, as experienced foremen and workers got tired of being told what to do and being forced to work overtime. Many retired or moved on, taking hundreds of years of cumulative experience with them. This "brain drain" later came back to bite AMF Harley.

FIX THIS FUCKING PLACE!

To its chagrin, AMF realized it would take more than adding a second shift to make twice as many motorcycles. "It didn't work because the processes were so screwed up," said Tom Gelb, who had rejoined Harley-Davidson as manufacturing engineering manager after the merger.

The brain drain exacerbated the problem by shifting too much responsibility to new people. That loss of experience was critical, according to Vaughn Beals, who was later

The 1971 FX Super Glide is considered one of the landmark designs of all time. It set the stage for future marketing trends.

Willie G. Davidson conceived the FX by stripping down an FL and then mounting the front end of an XL to it. Thus, the FX designation.

president of the company: "The new people tried making everything according to the prints. All the experienced people knew that 'you don't make them to the prints; you do this, and it works.'"

Before long, quality fell victim to the production push, and so did good relations between management and the workers. So, after ten years of peace at H-D, the workers struck for twenty-five days. On both sides, the whole experience had a hardening effect on attitudes that would later hound the company.

Despite all those problems, the company cranked out more than 34,000 Big Twins and Sportsters for 1972, a 50 percent increase.

Harley was busting at the seams, AMF was pushing for even greater production, and more problems surfaced every day. It got so bad that John O'Brien called Tom Gelb into his office and screamed at him, "Fix this fucking place!"

THE MILWAUKEE HOG BECOMES "YORK PORK"

Fix the fucking place meant moving assembly out of the decrepit Juneau factory. "Harley had run out of space," remembered Gelb, "so we put together a plan to build a new plant [next to the Capitol Drive plant] to build 75,000 motorcycles a year." Unfortunately, that plan was doomed because, Gelb continued, "AMF didn't like bricks and mortar."

Shortly after proposing the new factory, Gelb was told by president John O'Brien, "This is between you and me. Pack your bags; you're going to York, Pennsylvania. We're going to move assembly to our plant there." Gelb went to York to assess the equipment and to set the factory up for motorcycle production. "Not much was usable," he remembered.

AMF's York plant was largely idle because the two products made there—munitions and automatic bowling-pin setters—were no longer in demand as the Vietnam war wound down and the bowling craze of the 1950s and 1960s died. On the surface the move made sense.

To Gelb and others in Milwaukee, though, the numbers didn't add up. Gelb remembered, "They put together the economics to justify the move, and they were total

going to buy Harley. Would you and the other managers consider a leveraged buyout?'
"I felt like a kid, because I understood conceptually what a leveraged buyout was, but I
had no idea of the numbers," Beals continued. Gary Ward had a neighbor who worked for
Citicorp, and he set up a meeting. Afterward, "Citicorp was hot to trot," according to Beals.

Beals got eleven of the other top execs and outside counsel Tim Hoelter together and
convinced them that if they could scrape together a million bucks among them, they
really could do it. It was tough, but they found the money. Some say that former president
William H. Davidson even helped by lending money to Willie G., his son.

That settled, Beals worked on securing the financing and finalizing the deal with AMF's
negotiator, Merlin Nelson, whom Beals described as "a stuffed shirt." Nelson wanted "in
the range of one to two million from us," he continued. "Naturally, they thought two, and
I thought one. We had to scrounge like hell to get a million bucks. There was no way we
were gonna get two million without bringing in more people."

Beals and Nelson reached an impasse over the million. Then, Nelson made a critical
mistake. "He accused me of duplicity," Beals explained. "And I don't take that well. I
bounced off the wall, and told him to shove the company and walked away."

Nelson later approached Beals about resuming talks. "That was my chance," said Beals.
"I asked him to cut our equity from $2 million to $1 million, and he agreed. The price we
settled on was nominally $71 million, about 25 cents on a dollar of revenue. You could
never buy a company for that today."

With a letter of intent signed, Beals and company flew home to Milwaukee to
triumphantly announce the buyback, which was consummated June 16, 1981.

By 1978, change was on the horizon. The year brought the first 80-inch FL, and within a few years, the company would be sold to a management group that would breathe new life into the name Harley-Davidson.

Willie G. continued to do his magic in the Styling Department, releasing the FXWG Wide Glide in 1980.

THE EAGLE SOARS ALONE

After a huge celebration of Harley-Davidson's independence in York, Beals, Willie G., Bleustein, and the other owners fired up their bikes for a triumphant ride to Milwaukee, stopping at every Harley dealership along the route. "Every one of them had a big cake and celebration," Beals said. "I never wanted to see a cake again."

During the ride back, president Charlie Thompson called Tom Gelb and promoted him to vice president in charge of operations. It was a move that would prove critical to the company's future.

The new owners were excited and apprehensive, because they knew the reality that awaited them in Milwaukee. They were obscenely in debt, the company's reputation was in tatters, the whole country was in recession, the company and its dealers were already overstocked with motorcycles they couldn't sell, and the motorcycle market was in a death spiral. The one positive aspect was that they could convincingly blame all the ills of the recent past on AMF, giving Harley-Davidson the opportunity of a fresh start.

LEARNING FROM THE COMPETITION

The whole team worked to pull Harley-Davidson together. Money was nonexistent, so only really high-priority projects, like fixing the Shovel's oil leaks and continuing development of the Evolution engine, got funded. Everybody looked for ways to save money.

Tom Gelb looked at Japanese manufacturing methods and immediately saw the potential of just-in-time inventory, statistical process control, and employee involvement techniques. Within a few months after the buyback, Gelb tried such techniques out in a pilot program and then expanded them gradually throughout the company.

Gelb's changes saved the company. In the long term, it was the key to improving quality. It was too late to help the 1981 model year, though, and sales fell to the lowest level since 1973. Disaster loomed unless Harley's managers could turn everything around—and quickly.

SILENT SPRING

Then came 1982, the year spring never sprung for the Motor Company.

"A semirecession had hit automotive earlier," remembered Tom Gelb, "and all of a sudden in March 1982, it hit us. At the time, the Japanese manufacturers had about eighteen months' worth of finished inventory in the country, and they were selling two-

and three-year-old bikes right out of the crate and discounting them, so the bottom fell out of the market.

"I remember we had a policy meeting, and in the next weeks we cut our production rate in half, laid off 40 percent of our workforce, and cut all the salaries of the officers by something like 12 percent and the salaried workforce by 10 percent."

DODGING BULLETS

If all that wasn't bad enough, Harley's production was now below the minimum level specified in the agreements with its lenders. Those banks were free to foreclose at any time.

Fortunately, they chose not to, and here's where Gelb's Japanese-inspired changes became key: they saved Harley $20 million in inventory costs for 1982. Said Vaughn Beals, "In essence, the cash freed up from inventory offset the operating loss for 1982. Absent from that, I'm sure our lenders would not have supported us."

How close was it? Engineer Dave Webster left Harley in 1982 after being told by a friend and fellow Kiwanis Club member who sat on the board of one of the banks that "Harley has about thirty days before they'll have to close the door. Beat the rush!"

With Gelb's help, Harley dodged the first of many bullets. The company survived, but production fell to just over 24,000 units, about half the total for 1981.

CAUGHT IN A CROSSFIRE

Harley's big losses for 1982 were the result of more than a recession and the company's still-poor-but-improving reputation for quality. Harley was caught in the crossfire of a grudge match between industry leader Honda and pushy rival Yamaha.

Yamaha had staked its corporate reputation on winning dominance from Honda in 1982. In turn, Honda staked its corporate honor on retaining the lead. Honda and Yamaha crashed together in the US market like two sumo giants, and starved-to-the-bone Harley was crushed between them. Chairman Vaughn Beals fought back. On September 1, 1982, he petitioned the ITC for relief.

The Wide Glide offered true custom-bike styling in a package that anyone could buy at authorized Harley-Davidson dealers.

The 1981 FLH Heritage reminded Harley enthusiasts of the company's past. It also helped redirect the company's marketing compass to take advantage of former models.

RONNIE TO THE RESCUE

As point man for the tariff battle, Vaughn Beals was the focus of scathing criticism from the motorcycling press and from the buyers of Japanese bikes. He never dreamed Harley-Davidson would actually win its case, but he started the action to "get us through to the spring." That is, spring of 1983, when the Evo engine was scheduled to debut.

What made the criticism so galling was that anyone could see Harley's charges had some merit. Unsold Yamahas and Hondas piled up and were blown out at ridiculous prices.

The ITC heard arguments on Harley's petition on November 30, 1981. Beals brought powerful friends to the meeting, including a congressman and a senator. The Japanese made a fatal error before the hearing even started. "They had one attorney represent four companies, which was tangible evidence of Japan Inc.," Beans said. "I can't conceive of anyone dumb enough to do that, but they were."

The ITC adjourned the hearing and deliberated for months before recommending tariffs of 45 percent on all Japanese motorcycles over 700cc (after the first 7,000 imported) the first year, with diminishing percentages in the following four years. On April 1, 1983, President Ronald Reagan signed the tariffs into law.

Overall, the tariff was more symbolic than directly helpful. Anticipating the possibility that they might lose, the Japanese had stepped up production and shipment of their large 1983 models to get them on shore before the tariff took effect. A few months later, the Japanese reworked all their 750s into tariff-evading 700s, and Honda and Kawasaki avoided tariffs on their larger models by shifting assembly to their US plants.

As a result, Harley's sales for 1983 were even worse than in 1982. Citicorp held off on foreclosure, but everyone involved knew that if there wasn't a real improvement in the situation soon, it was all going to fold.

THE END OF THE SHOVELHEAD ROAD

It was the spring of 1983, and the Evo motor was ready for introduction in the 1984 line. Vaughn Beals and the cash-strapped company had to wonder, "What if big problems surfaced with the Evo? Should we bet this whole year's production that it would be trouble-free and accepted?" Because of lessons learned from its history, Harley-Davidson made a sensible compromise: it decided to keep the old engine in production, just along with the new one.

By keeping the old Shovelhead engine in production, H-D had a fallback in case the Evo bombed. At the same time, the company had something to offer both the traditionalist and the hoped-for newer buyers, giving both reasons to believe in the new Harley-Davidson.

To those who wanted modern refinement, Harley would offer the new Evo motor in its newer, rubber-mounted chassis. To the traditionalist, Harley would offer the Shovel motor in its solid-mount, twin-shock FLH and FX chassis.

The Evo was a hit, and that meant curtains for the Shovel. The final batch of Shovels—last-edition FLHXs—supposedly left the line in June 1984, and that was the end for both the grand old Shovelhead engine and for the real—that is, solid-mount, four-speed—Electra Glide.

The FXB Sturgis was a favorite from the beginning when it was launched in 1980. Its final year in the lineup was 1982, before returning again in 1991.

CHAPTER 7

THE EVOLUTION ERA

BY GREG FIELD

THE EVOLUTION ENGINE MARKED THE MOTOR COMPANY'S EMERGENCE FROM THE DARK AGES OF THE AMF SHOVELHEAD ERA INTO HARLEY-DAVIDSON'S RENAISSANCE. THAT RENAISSANCE OFFICIALLY BEGAN IN LATE SUMMER 1983, WHEN HARLEY INTRODUCED ANOTHER UPDATE TO ITS OHV BIG TWIN ENGINE. THIS TIME, THE NEW ENGINE EVEN CAME WITH AN OFFICIAL NAME: V² EVOLUTION.

True to Vaughn Beals's quote, when the Evolution came out, the dealers and buyers recognized that this, by God, *was* a new engine. No more 600 miles to the quart of oil. No more parts rattling off. No more breakdowns on every ride. The Evo was reliable and oil-tight, and at the same time it was still, by God, a *Harley* engine. Same great sound. Same good vibes. Same indefinable mystique.

From that, the dealers and buyers and even moto-magazine scribes began to recognize that this, by God, was a new *Motor Company*. Before the Evo, Harley-Davidson and its motorcycles were the laughingstock of a niche market; by the end of the Evolution era, Harley-Davidson's methods were studied in business schools and its motorcycles were objects of mainstream lust around the world.

That transformation didn't happen overnight, and Harley-Davidson nearly went under doing it. And it didn't begin in 1983 either.

DAWN OF THE EVO ERA

The first glimmer of a new dawn for the Motor Company came in April 1976, at a management retreat at the Pinehurst Country Club in North Carolina. There, Vaughn Beals, Jeff Bleustein, Willie G., and others put together the plan for Harley's future.

"The basic plan that came out of Pinehurst was, 'Let's ride two horses at once.'" according to Vaughn Beals. "We needed two powertrains. One was the Evolution engine, and the other was a modern water-cooled V-configuration family of engines, code-named Nova, that would allow us to compete with everybody else."

At the time, Harley was short on money and engineering might, so why not concentrate on one powerplant? "We all felt the V-twin was our history—that it would have been stupid to abandon it," Beals explained. "That's what Indian did, and it bankrupted the company! And deep down we all hoped that the V-twin would be our future too, but we were looking at much more sophisticated water-cooled engines from our competitors, so we also felt that having the V-twin as a sole product strategy of the company was too risky at that time."

On their return from the retreat, they fleshed out their plan and calculated the cost. By September of 1976, the plan was ready. "We figured it was gonna cost $100 million," Beals remembered, "which was bigger money back then than it is now. I had looked at the prior strategic product plans that had been submitted, and . . . the numbers were like a third of what we came up with. To go in and tell the boss that the price tag is three times what he thought it was going to be is not something we contemplated with pleasure."

AMF'S "LONG, COLD SHOWER"

When Beals presented the new plan to AMF senior management, "it was a long, cold shower for them," he remembered. "AMF never really understood Harley-Davidson. They didn't understand long lead time, capital intensive stuff because it doesn't take five years to develop a new pair of skies or a tennis racket."

AMF wanted a third party to look at the plan Beals presented, so it hired the Boston Consulting Group (BCG). BCG did an extensive study, surveying dealers and customers in depth. "They endorsed our plan and said that what we proposed was a reasonable thing to do," Beals said. With BCG's endorsement and AMF's money, in early 1977 work began on the planned update of the Big Twin and Sportster engines, the new liquid-cooled engines, and several new chassis.

BUILDING A "FIRST ENGINEERING DEPARTMENT"

The plan called for reworking the Big Twin engine in-house and contracting out the water-cooled engine, with a planned debut for both engines in the early 1980s and an updated Sportster engine to follow. Why not do both in-house? "The fundamental problem was that in 1976 we didn't have the first Engineering Department," Beals explained. "We needed to make the Nova engine from scratch. Thinking that we could make one from scratch and simultaneously develop two new engines—I don't think that would have been good judgment."

Harley-Davidson plant on West Juneau Avenue in Milwaukee, 1990s.

The release of the Evolution V2 engine allowed Harley to launch new models, including the 1984 FXRT. The aerodynamic fairing was a spinoff of the ill-fated Nova project from a few years before.

With that, Bleustein began building Harley's "first Engineering Department" and selecting a firm to design the other engine. One of Bleustein's key acquisitions was a new leader for the powertrain section, Don Valentine. Valentine's first efforts were focused on improving the Shovelhead, but later he played a key role in designing the Evo. Eventually, Harley-Davidson picked Porsche Design to pen the Nova engine.

HANK HUBBARD AND "THE CONCEPT"

In November 1977, engineer Hank Hubbard began work on an updated Harley engine. The basic assignment? "Redesign the engine from the crankcases up—for state-of-the-art oil control, to increase the bore to get more power, and for cost reduction," Hubbard remembered.

At the time, Hubbard was Harley's main engine concept man—the guy who brainstormed the fundamentals of future designs. True to form, Hubbard came up with a design concept by the end of November that remained largely intact as the Evo.

Although Hubbard finished the concept drawing, he said, "two other guys gave birth to it, Bob Sroka and Dave Webster."

EARLY EVOLUTION

As the whole design evolved over the next two years, the name stayed the same. "We referred to it as 'Evolution' from the start," remembered engineer Bob Sroka. "It's just one of those things that seemed like it was always there."

Before long, prototype Evo-powered bikes were tearing up the local roads. "A lot of the durability testing was being done locally when we began, on the streets around Milwaukee," added engineer Dave Webster. "I had a personally assigned prototype for my own use. When we were about halfway through the program, we switched to road and high-speed testing at the track at Talladega [Alabama]."

TEAM EVO

Sroka and Webster completed the foundation design work by 1980, but thousands of additional details still needed to be finalized. "Through the Evolution engine, we wanted to get back the customer base we were losing because of the problems with the Shovelhead," Don Valentine said. "The engine had to be leak free and relatively trouble free—we were looking for a 100,000-mile engine. And we had to do it on a shoestring budget. Money was very tight—especially in the 1980s."

Using what money it did have, a whole team of engineers from the powertrain section got to work under chief Valentine.

Over the next three years of slaving over hot dynos, in front of glowing computer terminals, and riding nearly 1,000,000 test miles, the Evo team refined the design for production. "We'd look at problems one at a time and grind them out," Valentine remembered. "Cylinder heads were the biggest challenge. There was a learning curve because the heads were all new. We even had to develop a new casting process for them."

Soon, a host of talented people from throughout the company joined the engineers from powertrain. "The Evolution project was a collaboration," explained Mark Tuttle, later vice president in charge of engineering. "It was really the beginning of the program to involve more people in the design and development of our products. Historically, the hand-off from engineering to manufacturing has sort of been, 'Here's the perfect design—now you figure out how to make it,' versus working in collaboration to balance manufacturing needs with functional needs with styling needs and so forth."

THE FINANCIAL SQUEEZE

If the budget had been shoestring in the late 1970s, two events during Evo design really screwed the money valve down tight.

The first was Vaughn Beals and a group of other executives buying Harley from AMF. Obscenely in debt, and no longer having corporate sugar daddy AMF to cover any shortfalls in revenue, Harley-Davidson could only spend what it made—and it wasn't making much. Sales for 1981 were the lowest in a decade. Despite that, Harley-Davidson put every dollar it could into completing the Evo for 1983 and even raised the bar on the design: "After the buyback, the decree was given that with the Evolution we would put the Harley engine back to its reputation before AMF took over," Bob Sroka said.

The second event that dried up funding was the bottom dropping out of the motorcycle market in 1982. Motorcycles of all makes were stacked up in warehouses. In response, Harley laid off nearly half its workforce, cut production by half, slashed salaries, and asked the US government for tariffs. Those cuts put production under levels specified in its loan agreements, meaning the bankers could foreclose at any time. "We were operating at the pleasure of the banks," said Tom Gelb, vice president in charge of operations.

Ultimately, a supportive banker, Gelb's productivity initiatives, and profits from building practice-bomb casings for the US Air Force kept Harley alive through 1982 and 1983.

The FXRT handled extremely well, helping to usher in a new concept of long-distance riding—sport touring.

WHEN THE MAGAZINE TEST REPORTS CAME IN, THEY WERE JUST THE SORT OF REVIEWS HARLEY NEEDED.

Near Copper Harbor on Lake Superior, Electra Glide Classic 1996 FLHTCI model.

DELAYED EVOLUTION

"I don't think we ever made a tougher decision than when we finally had to delay the Evolution," Beals said. "We had planned to introduce it at the start of model year 1983, but the one vow we took because of the reputation we had was that when the Evolution engine came out, it would be durable, oil-tight, bulletproof.

"We finally decided that the 1983 model introduction was too risky because we weren't yet confident that it was bulletproof—so we reluctantly decided to delay the introduction until Daytona, which is in March, halfway through the model season. As time went on, we decided to put it off for a whole calendar year. Man, we needed it badly at that time because the market was terrible, which meant we needed the engine sooner rather than later."

The few engineers who hadn't been laid off used the extra time well, devising fixes for the problems that originally delayed production, and refining the tooling and processes for manufacture. One good thing that came out of the delay was the Evo's ingenious three-piece rocker cover. Once unbolted, the three pieces slide off the heads like cards from a deck, leaving room to remove the heads and cylinders while the engine is still in the frame.

When Beals and company decided the form of the 1984 lineup, they had to decide whether the Shovelhead would go out of production at the end of 1983 in favor of the Evo, or whether both would be built. In the end, Harley-Davidson decided to keep the old engine in production, along with the new one.

NEW GUTS FOR OLD GLORY: DEBUT OF THE EVOLUTION ENGINE

When the Evo was finally released in late summer 1983, Harley billed it as "New Guts for Old Glory" in a special brochure that exhorted the faithful and all those who'd been sitting on the fence to come ride it in Harley's Super Ride program.

For those who wanted modern refinement, Harley offered the new Evo motor in its newer, rubber-mounted chassis: the FLT, FLHT, and FXR. For the traditionalist, Harley would offer the Shovel motor in its solid-mount, twin-shock FLH and FX chassis. For those who wanted a little modern and a lot of tradition, Harley offered up an all-new model, the FXST Softail.

When the magazine test reports came in, they were just the sort of reviews Harley needed. *Cycle* magazine tested an FXRT in the November 1983 issue and raved, "In one 1,000-mile trip, the engine consumed about 12 ounces of oil, and only a slight amount of oil mist weeped from the clutch-actuating arm. It never leaked a drop while in our hands."

Motorcyclist magazine (January 1984) also tested the Evo-powered FXRT and was similarly pleased: "For those who wanted to see if Harley could build a real, honest-to-Davidson 1984 motorcycle, feast your eyes. The '84 season is here—and Harley is right here with it."

That same issue of *Motorcyclist* also named Vaughn Beals as 1983's Motorcyclist of the Year. Because of his handling of the whole tariff issue, plus the astonishing resurgence of Harley-Davidson in late 1983, Beals was the unanimous choice of the magazine's editors for the award. This was just the kind of publicity the company needed in the months following the Evo introduction. Sales continued to rise and even held through the winter months.

After the great reception of the Evos and increased sales, times were better at the Motor Company, but they were still far from good. Needing every sale it could get, Harley

released a limited edition model, the FXRDG Disc Glide. The bike's disc rear wheel and chrome engine castings gave a glimpse of Harley's future. The other surprise was a new wet clutch. It worked well and had a much lighter pull, courtesy of the diaphragm spring that replaced the coil springs in the old clutch.

Even though the alloy-based Evo engine represented a big step forward in terms of technology, Harley-Davidson didn't forget its past, as represented here by the 1988 FXSTS Softail.

EVOLUTION IN BLUE

With the excellent FXR chassis and the reliable new Evo motor, Harley released the FXRP Pursuit Glide and roared off in a high-speed pursuit of the 600-pound gorilla of the police-motorcycle business: the California Highway Patrol (CHP).

Harley convinced the CHP to test the FXRP against the Kawasakis they had been buying since the mid-1970s. After exhaustive testing, the CHP approved the FXRP, and Harley began taking business away from Kawasaki. The CHP bought 152 in 1984. The Chippies liked their new Hogs, so they ordered another 161 in 1985. Other departments did too, and Harley was once again a major player in the police business.

Long before the 1984 model year ended, Beals and company knew they had a winner. The Evo-powered models were selling at record pace. Everyone loved the Evolution because it looked and sounded like a Harley, but it didn't leak or burn enough oil to cause concern, didn't need much more maintenance than a car engine, and it didn't rattle itself apart.

Harley started an aggressive licensing program that paid off big time in the years ahead. The first visible product of that effort was Harley-Davidson beer (brewed by Pabst). In later years, Harley licensed everything from basketball shoes to cigarettes.

When all was tallied at the end of the year, Harley's domestic sales were up 31 percent, to 38,741—a phenomenal increase in a year in which the US motorcycle market descended deeper into a sales slump that would continue through the 1980s. Evo-fueled

ABOVE: The 1990 FLSTF Fat Boy broke new styling trends, making it one of the best-selling models in the lineup for many years. It remains a favorite today.

BELOW: Heritage Softail Classic 1997 FLSTC model along Mississippi River in Minnesota across from Trempeleau Mountain—"the mountain that soaks in the water."

sales increases elevated the Motor Company to third place in the US motorcycle market in the over-850cc class, behind Honda and Yamaha.

When Harley announced its 1985 Big Twin line, it was all-Evo. The old Electra Glide was gone, but the FX models were back, powered by the Evo engine.

The real news for 1985 was in the final drive, because even the five-speed models were fitted with rubber-belt final drive. Vaughn Beals said, "We just wanted something you didn't have to oil or adjust, that didn't spray oil all over you. We got that, but the belts also lasted much longer and looked better too."

Now, it's difficult to imagine a Harley with any other type of drive.

Sales of the Evo Big Twins were up again for 1985, in a year of massive losses for everyone else in the industry. Harley's share increased to put it in second place, behind only Honda in the over-850cc class.

A NEAR-DEATH EXPERIENCE

At the end of Harley-Davidson's first century, who could question that the company is a survivor? The Ford Model T, Great Depression, World War II, British invasion, Japanese invasion, breakup of the clan, hostile takeover attempt, AMF, market crash of the 1980s—you've read about them all and how they each nearly killed the company.

As damaging as they were, previous crises were nothing compared to the nail-biter of 1985. And ironically, it was Harley's Evo-powered successes that sparked the new crisis.

During the darkest days of the early 1980s, Citicorp could have pulled the plug any time but didn't because Harley's loan officer, Jack Reilly, was confident Vaughn Beals and company would prevail. But Citicorp also kept supporting Harley because it thought it stood a better chance of recovering the loan by keeping Harley alive than by killing it while it was down.

That all changed in 1984, when Harley began looking like a comeback kid and when Jack Reilly took another job and was replaced by a loan officer who had opposed lending money to Harley in the first place. Citicorp believed another recession was imminent and

that Harley would not survive it. Without Reilly to plead Harley's case, Citicorp decided to pull the plug and liquidate Harley before the crash.

Citicorp passed its death sentence in November 1984 by telling Harley the bank would cut off all over-advances in March 1985. "We made money in 1984, but without continuing over-advances, we were dead," Vaughn Beals explained. "We didn't yet have the money to operate and pay off all the loans."

On further reflection, Citicorp figured the best month to liquidate Harley would be the end of November, so in March the bank extended over-advance privileges to carry Harley-Davidson into October. That brief reprieve meant that Harley-Davidson would have to find a new lender and close the deal by December 31, 1985, or file for Chapter 11 bankruptcy.

All through the summer, Beals and Chief Financial Officer Rich Teerlink looked for another lender to save the company, but were rejected because all the banks thought there must be a catch. If Harley was making a profit, regaining market share, and getting steadily more efficient, why was Citibank bailing? Try as they might, Beals and Teerlink couldn't convince other bankers that Citibank just wanted out—even if that meant destroying a now-viable Motor Company. With time running out, Beals started preparing to file for Chapter 11 bankruptcy.

When it was just about too late, Rich Teerlink found a couple of new heroes who helped save the company. The first was Steve Deli of Dean Witter Reynolds. Deli introduced Teerlink to the other savior, Bob Koe, a Harley-riding banker at Heller Financial. Koe liked Teerlink's pitch and the idea of helping the Motor Company, so he got the deal rolling and set up a meeting with Heller's chief, Norm Blake.

By the time Heller had investigated Harley's finances and was ready to discuss details, it was late December, leaving no time to find another savior if this deal fell through. Beals, Teerlink, and Operations Vice President Tom Gelb made their do-or-die pitch on the morning of December 23. They laid out all the numbers, showing how Harley had improved in every way. Like all the other bankers, though, Blake didn't believe Citicorp wouldn't bail out if things were really that rosy, so he rejected the deal.

The 1991 FXDB Sturgis not only marked the return of a favorite factory custom, but it also paved the way for a new frame design—the Dyna. The Dyna relied on CAD technology to lay out its frame tube geometry.

Ironically, in a nod to the 50th anniversary of Daytona Bike Week, Harley produced a special edition of the FXDB Sturgis, presenting it as the "Daytona."

Lesser men would have given up then and gone home for the holidays, but not Beals, Teerlink, and Gelb. Instead, they convinced Bob Koe to beg another meeting that afternoon with Blake.

Incredibly, Koe came through, and with Deli as go-between, the Harley executives negotiated terms progressively more advantageous for Heller until Blake finally approved the deal.

Normally, the signing of papers and transferring money to close the deal would have been mere formality. In this case, it was the holiday season, leaving just a few business days to get it all done on the 31st. Naturally, everything that could go wrong did, and the 31st became the longest day of Rich Teerlink's life. Several times that day one of the parties told him it couldn't get its part done in time. Through force of will, he exhorted each to exert themselves on a holiday, completing the last transaction with just minutes left before bankruptcy. If any man deserved a drink that New Year's Eve, it was Rich Teerlink.

"We still operated at the pleasure of the banks," Tom Gelb explained, "but at least we had breathing room and weren't paying this tremendous amount of interest on the over-advances."

SOFTAIL CUSTOM AND HERITAGE

While the refinancing drama played out, Harley introduced its 1986 line. The Softail line was updated with a new frame and five-speed transmission, which meant the end of the line for the old four-speed with its kick-starter. "We had a major insurrection over that," Beals remembered, "but the company decided 'to hell with it' and just ignored the complaints."

The Softail line also split to include a glitzier sibling: the Softail Custom. The most notable features of the Softail Custom were its disc-type rear wheel, black-and-chrome engine, and a frame painted to match the tanks and fenders. The high-priced Custom was Harley's bestseller that year.

Midyear, Harley introduced the FLST Heritage Softail, which flaunted a fat front end styled after those of the 1950s Hydra-Glides. The Heritage was another masterpiece from the Styling Department and an even more audacious future-from-the-past trick than they'd pulled off with the original Softail. *Cycle* called it a "machine of arresting simplicity" and "the most elegant Harley-Davidson of its generation." Like the original Softail before it, the Heritage was a hit its first year and later spawned its own distinct model line.

If you were one of "the few among millions" who wanted your new Harley with a four-speed tranny and a kicker, the Wide Glide was your only choice for 1986. Last of the old-frame Big Twins, the Wide Glide was clearly reaching an evolutionary dead end, but sales had doubled during its first year in Evo form, so the Evo Wide Glide was certainly deserving of one last limited run.

In a final and fond nod to its heritage, the final edition Wide Glide was available with (and without) the flamed tank graphics that had made the original so striking. The new Fog Candy Red flames blazed over the Candy Burgundy of the rest of the bodywork.

Once the 1,000 or so copies Harley built were all sold, that was it. As for the Wide Glide model, it would rise once again in the 1990s like a phoenix out of the metallic flames on the final edition's tanks.

GOING PUBLIC

Less than six months after Heller Financial's last-second save of the company from bankruptcy, Harley-Davidson confounded all expectations by going public—selling its stock on the NASDAQ stocks exchange. "When Steve Deli from Dean Witter told us we should go public, we all said, 'You're crazy!'" Tom Gelb remembered. "But he was right. From then on, we controlled our own destiny."

After the sale and paying off bankers, Beals and company were free to run Harley-Davidson without interference from bankers, and they actually had cash on hand for the first time. Deli convinced Harley-Davidson to use the money to diversify, so in December 1986 the Motor Company bought Holiday Rambler, a manufacturer of motor homes. That acquisition doubled the size and earnings base of Harley-Davidson, Inc.

As the motorcycle market continued its long crash, Harley-Davidson was the only motorcycle company in the world to increase sales in 1986. Its share of the over-850cc market was now one-third, neck and neck with Honda.

To celebrate the 10th anniversary of the Low Rider, Willie G. and Louie Netz created a new model for those who wanted the comfort of rubber mounts with all their chrome and polish: the FXLR (Low Rider) Custom.

The Custom featured a 21-inch front wheel and skinny tire, a slim fender, a chrome bullet headlamp, chrome triple clamps, a hand-laced leather strap down the center of the tank, and special two-tone paint and striping. Harley was justly proud of the new Custom and featured it in full-size poster form on the flip side of a fold-up brochure. It sold well its first year, but then sales declined steadily until it was canceled at the end of 1994.

Harley scored a public relations coup on March 17, 1987, when it petitioned the ITC (International Trade Commission) to end the tariff on Japanese big bikes, and on May 16, 1987, President Ronald Reagan visited the York, Pennsylvania, assembly plant and gave a speech praising Harley's fast recovery.

RIDING WALL STREET AND TAKING THE LEAD

By early 1987, Harley-Davidson was healthy enough to qualify for listing on the New York Stock Exchange (NYSE). To celebrate its first day of trading on the NYSE, Vaughn Beals, Rich Teerlink, and Willie G. thundered down Wall Street on July 1, 1987, leading a procession that included a semi and trailer painted in Harley colors.

Newspaper accounts of the landmark event noticed that Willie G. even wore a necktie, which some said was the first time since Ronald Reagan visited York. In a possibly related event, Harley began licensing its trademarks to a tie maker.

Year-end tallies gave Harley-Davidson another reason to celebrate: its 38 percent market share in the over-850cc category made it the industry leader for the first time in nearly a decade.

By 1988, the tough times were finally becoming good times for the Motor Company. Though the US motorcycle market was down 28 percent, Harley's sales were up by nearly 14 percent, surpassing 40,000 for the first time since the crash of the US motorcycle market in 1982. Celebrity converts began showing up everywhere (even in the 1988 Harley catalog) on their Harleys, raising Harley's profile as an American icon.

And midyear, Harley released a new icon, the FXSTS Springer Softail, created by bolting up to the Softail a modernized version of the Harley's old springer front end. "I loved the idea because it gave us a way to attract new customers and screw the Japanese because they didn't have anything like it in their heritage to go back to," Vaughn Beals exclaimed. "The only problem was that making it happen took longer than any of us would like to have seen."

It took longer because at first they couldn't figure out how to get modern durability out of the bearings on the fork rockers. "Remember," said Chief Engineer Don Valentine, "the old rockers at the bottom of the forks had bushings and grease fittings. No matter what you did, those bushings would wear out and get sloppy real fast."

The FXST Softail platform first rolled in 1984. By 1995, various models, including the FXSTSB Bad Boy, composed its lineup.

Eventually, they found a Teflon bearing that could do the job, but new problems surfaced during pilot production. "It was a real bitch to make!" Tom Gelb explained. "With that mechanical setup, there were a million parts, and I mean they were all polished and chromed. It was a very labor-intensive process. At the time, we were just hoping we wouldn't sell too many of them."

Complementing the chrome front end were the slimmer (3.5-gallon) Fat Bob tanks, black paint with red and yellow pinstripes, the blacked-out and chromed engine from the Softail Custom, and 85th anniversary tank graphics. All 1,300 numbered copies of this limited edition classic sold out almost instantly.

BEALS BOWS OUT

In March, leader of the pack Vaughn Beals stepped down and left the Motor Company in the capable hands of Rich Teerlink, the new CEO. Beals stayed on as chairman of the board.

To show how Harley prospered under Beals's leadership, consider these numbers: in 1989 when he left, the overall market for street bikes in the United States was down by 28 percent compared to the previous year and had dropped by two-thirds compared to 1981, when he led the buyback. Despite that, Harley's sales were up by 17 percent for the year, and total production of Big Twins and Sportsters topped 55,000, the highest total in company history.

Another new trend: sales figures began to reflect Harley-Davidson's production capacity more than the actual demand, and waiting lists became the norm for the most popular models.

ABOVE: Throughout the years, the FLSTF Fat Boy has changed little. The bike is best recognized for its dished aluminum wheels and fat body panels.

BELOW: Road King 1997 model FLHR with model TLE sidecar.

Students of Harley-Davidson's history and heritage know that the FLSTS is a modern Softail, launched in 1997. But to the untrained eye, it can look suspiciously like the first Panhead of 1948.

Harley released a new Softail for 1990, the FLSTF Fat Boy, a production replica of the custom Heritage Softail ridden to Daytona by Willie G. in 1988.

By design, Fat Boy had the tough look of bolts and rivets and aluminum plate. In fact, the only parts soft and humanistic about it were the pigskin seat with hand-laced detailing on the seat valance and the hand-laced leather tank trim. It was, as the ad said, "a heavy-duty hunk of style."

What's in this name? Well, the atomic bombs dropped on Japan were code named "Fat Man" and "Little Boy." Some say the Fat Boy name is a combination of the two and the bike's silver-on-silver look was inspired by the sleek silver B-29 Superfortresses that dropped those bombs. And the new Fat Boy insignia on the tank looks suspiciously like a few US Army Air Force unit insignias during the war.

Also in 1990, Harley enthusiasts mourned the passing of the company's best customer and perhaps most flamboyant booster, Malcolm Forbes, who died on February 24.

While the FXR models were darlings of the motorcycle press, they were never popular among Harley's more conservative fans, because the FXRs looked too "foreign." When the FXR series finally replaced the classic FXs, these guys let Harley know just how unhappy they were. To its credit, Harley listened and put extraordinary effort into correcting the problem by creating a new chassis designed from the start to have the FX look.

After an early brainstorming session with the marketing and styling folks, lead engineer Rit Booth left with a slogan that would carry him through the design process: "What the customer wants is a bike that looks like an FX. And this next part is very precisely worded: if it doesn't vibrate, that's OK." Nothing else mattered as much as making it look like the old FX models—not rubber mounts, not stiffness of the frame, not handling qualities, not comfort, not anything. But, if they could get the look *and* still squeeze in rubber mounts, they should go for it.

The look boiled down to long and low, or low and long, because one helps create the illusion of the other. So Booth and his team stretched and lowered whatever they could. When they were done, almost every part was new, including crankcases, the transmission case, and the primary covers. But in the end, Booth and the other engineers on the team got both the look *and* the rubber mounts.

For 1991, the new bike was released as the limited-edition Dyna Glide Sturgis. Even with all the updates, the new Sturgis looked almost identical to the original Sturgis. As in black on black. Orange highlights on the tank, timer cover, wheels, and elsewhere. Low bars on high risers for the drag-bike look, without the backache. It even got the old-style, dual-strut Sportster front fender, as on the original Sturgis.

It was another in a string of winners. And it was the start of a whole new line of Dyna Glide models that soon replaced the FXRs.

Nineteen ninety-three marked the company's 90th anniversary and a cause for celebration. Harley released special anniversary editions of most models and invited everyone to join the celebration in Milwaukee in June. Over 100,000 of the faithful made the pilgrimage.

The new FLSTN Heritage Softail Nostalgia anchored the anniversary line. Willie G. based the new machine on the Fat Boy but added fishtail mufflers, "fat gangster whitewalls" on laced wheels, and a seat and bags with black-and-white Holstein-fur inserts. Paintwork carried through the Holstein theme—Birch White with Vivid Black panels on both tanks and fenders, with red and gray pinstriping.

Naturally enough, the Nostalgia took on several appropriate nicknames, including "Moo Glide," "Cow Glide," and "Heritage Holstein." And all 2,700 numbered copies sold out quicker than you could tip a cow.

Harley's factory chopper—the Wide Glide—returned in Dyna guise for 1993. Since the Dyna was designed from the start to mimic the look of the old FX chassis, it was a natural base for an updated Wide Glide.

"WHAT THE CUSTOMER WANTS IS A BIKE THAT LOOKS LIKE AN FX. AND THIS NEXT PART IS VERY PRECISELY WORDED: IF IT DOESN'T VIBRATE, THAT'S OK."

Change the color of a bike and that can completely alter its demeanor. That's what Harley stylists did with the FLSTS for 1998.

Just as Harley fans missed the look of the FX models, they also missed the look of the old FLH Electra Glide. Harley first tried to re-create it by stripping the fairing off the FLHT, but the upper fork and headlight area never looked right, and it didn't have the speedo on the tank-mounted dash, where Bill Harley had decreed it should be. Harley finally got it right for 1994, with the FLHR Electra Glide Road King.

END OF THE FXR LINE

By 1994, Dynas had replaced all the FXR models except the basic FXR Super Glide (the lowest-cost Big Twin) and the FXLR (Low Rider) Custom. At the end of this year, these last two were cut, and the FXR chassis was put out to pasture, but not permanently, as we'll see.

For 1997, Willie G. and Louie N. unveiled their latest rendition of a Harley idea whose time had never really passed, the FLSTS Heritage Softail Springer. Basically, it was another front-end trick. First, they modified the Springer front end and fender to fit a fat 16-inch front wheel and topped it off with a chrome horn just like the original. Then they added a tombstone taillight, whitewall tires, and a big saddle with outsized tooled-leather skirts, chromed dual exhaust with fishtail mufflers, and fringed, tooled-leather bags. The result was an almost spot-on re-creation of the pimped-up bikes the bobber guys of the 1940s and 1950s derided as "garbage wagons."

While the FXSTS resembles the early Panheads, the FLHR Road King, such as this 1998 model, could serve as a stand-in for a Duo-Glide.

By the late 1990s, fashion in the custom circles had gone from the tall, slim chopper to the long, fat, and low lead sled look. For 1998, Willie G. presented his own rendition of that look—the FLTR Road Glide—simultaneously creating the factory custom bagger and a successful new model. The Road Glide's frame-mounted fairing was based on that of the FLT, but it was chopped and lowered and given some attitude, and a very low windscreen.

For 1999, the Twin Cam 88 replaced the Evolution engine in most Big Twin models. The Softails remained the only regular production Harleys still powered by the Evolution powerplant.

The limited-edition FXR^2 and FXR^3 released in 1999 were the only other models that retained the Evolution engine. The FXR^2 and FXR^3 were the first factory super customs—chrome-covered beauties that were all-Harley, yet as customized as any bike on the bike show circuit. All that was really missing was a custom exhaust, but the factory couldn't supply that and still remain in good graces with the EPA.

For 2000 came the FXR^4, which was the last of two distinguished breeds: the last of the rubber-mounted FXR models and the last of the Evo-powered Harley Big Twins.

THE EVO'S EPITAPH

Between the production capacity increase Harley gained every year and the continued increase in demand, Harley took the US sales lead during the Evolution Big Twin's last year, and not just in the over-850cc category. Combined sales of the Big Twins and Sportsters surpassed the US sales of the whole Honda line for the first time since the early 1960s. That's the best possible send-off for the engine that made it all possible to get to this point—the Evolution Big Twin.

ABOVE: As its name suggests, the FXSTB Night Train looks good in black. The tins are gloss black and the engine cases wear a wrinkle black finish.

BELOW: This 1998 FXDWG Dyna Wide Glide sports the company's 95th anniversary paint scheme.

CHAPTER 8

THE TWIN CAM ERA

BY STEVE ANDERSON

HARLEY-DAVIDSON IS ABOUT AS PARSIMONIOUS WHEN IT COMES TO DOLING
OUT NEW ENGINES AS AN IRS AUDITOR IS ABOUT GIVING REBATES. THE
SPORTSTER POWERPLANT DEBUTED IN 1957—BUT AS AN OVERHEAD-VALVE
ADAPTATION OF THE KH FLATHEAD THAT APPEARED IN 1952, ITSELF CLOSELY
RELATED TO A NON-UNIT CONSTRUCTION MOTOR INTRODUCED IN 1937.
EVEN THAT ENGINE WAS BASED ON AN EARLIER POWERPLANT INTRODUCED
IN 1929. THE FIRST OF THE OVERHEAD-VALVE BIG TWINS, THE EL61—OR
KNUCKLEHEAD—WAS BIRTHED BY BILL HARLEY AND THE OTHERS IN 1936.
IN AN EVOLUTIONARY PROBLEM-SOLVING PROCESS, THE KNUCKLEHEAD LED
TO THE PANHEAD, THE PANHEAD LED TO THE SHOVELHEAD, AND IN 1984, THE
SHOVELHEAD GAVE WAY TO THE BLOCKHEAD, OR EVOLUTION. BUT EVEN AFTER
ALL THOSE CHANGES, A REINCARNATED BILL HARLEY WOULD STILL HAVE BEEN
ABLE TO RECOGNIZE HIS HANDIWORK IN THE EVO BIG TWIN. HE WOULD EVEN
RECOGNIZE SOME OF THE PARTS.

So when the Twin Cam 88 debuted in 1998—the first completely Big Twin since 1936—it was the biggest news Harley had since the first of Franklin Roosevelt's four terms in office. The motorcycle press hurried to describe the new powerplant, to tell of the improvements and quantify its performance. But in all the talk about power and technology, performance and reliability, camshafts and oil systems, not all that much has been said about the Twin Cam's roots, about how it came to be, or about how this new Big Twin took exactly the form and shape it did. If you're familiar with Harley's increasingly corporate look, you might expect the beginning of that history to be the result of plans laid out by some buttoned-down product planners and marketing experts in some fluorescent-lit conference room in that old red brick building on Milwaukee's Juneau Avenue. But you'd be wrong.

Try instead Zorba's, a funky family-owned restaurant (Greek, of course) where some midlevel Motor Company managers liked to get together on Saturday mornings. Bruce Dennert, powertrain design manager, was one of the Harley folks there in the spring of 1992. "There was Bill Schultz, manager of the Softail," Dennert said. "Scott Miller, marketing guy; Hugh Vallely, office of program manager; and myself. The whole idea was to get Scott Miller—the marketing guy—to buy breakfast."

Expensing the breakfast wasn't totally illegitimate, Dennert points out: "We used to talk product. That morning we were talking about the problems and limitations with the Evo. We said you had to do something new or better, and we sketched out on a napkin what we should do to enhance the Big Twin family. Meanwhile there was some long-range planning going on in the company, and one of the goals was to do the traditional product as long as we could legally."

ABOVE: The big news for 1998 was the addition of another camshaft for Big Twin engines, as on this Road King. Enter the Twin Cam 88, an engine that displaced an additional 8 cubic inches over the single-cam Evolution V2.

BELOW: The 2000 Softail line was issued a proprietary Twin Cam 88 engine that had internal rotating counterbalancers to subdue vibration to the rider. The FXSTD Deuce was also new for 2000.

The 2004 Softail model lineup included the Fat Boy. All Softails utilized carburetors unless customers ordered the optional electronic sequential port fuel injection.

That napkin and the sketch on it set wheels in motion. After further Saturday discussions at Zorba's, the idea of an enhanced, yet traditional, Big Twin gained ground. A meeting was set up at Harley. Miller, Dennert, and Vallely represented the Zorba regulars, along with some new additions. Don Keiffer came from manufacturing engineering (he was one of the two technical managers of the Capitol Drive plant who actually built engines), and Willie G. was the representative of styling and, well, tradition.

According to Keiffer, the first question that came up was: "Do we do a Nova-type project (Harley's never-produced, Porsche-designed water-cooled V-4 from the early 1980s) or do we stick to the tried and true?" Tried and true won easily, and with significant urging from Willie G., the group came up with a specification list for what was called "The Classic Engine Project." It was just five items long. Any new engine, they decided, should:

- be a 45-degree V-twin
- use air cooling
- have pushrods rather than overhead cams
- place its cylinders inline, rather than offset
- look like an Evo from 25 feet away

Keiffer remembers some polarization: "[Engine designer] Dennert pushed for more innovation, while Willie G. said, 'Do anything you want as long as we have that spec list.'"

Dennert, reasonably enough, wanted more: "A new Big Twin had to be better than an Evo; it had to give our customers a reason to buy a new one, to relight the passion that was already there."

In additional meetings, the Classic Engine Project was further defined. Mark Tuttle, vice president in charge of engineering, presented the project to Motor Company executives at a strategy planning retreat called Pinehurst II in North Carolina. The location carried historical weight, because the decision to go with traditional powerplants instead of the Nova water-cooled V-4 had been made at Pinehurst, more than a decade earlier. The meeting produced a preliminary go-ahead for the Classic Engine. Dennert, then acting chief of powerplants, started with five engineers to flesh out the specifications. In the spring and summer of 1992, Keiffer remembered, the project came together: "We wanted to strengthen the whole lower end; people with hot rods were breaking crankcases. The idea was to leave the Evo top end alone, and slide new cases under it." In many ways, the project at the time was seen simply as an evolution of the Evo, another incremental step on the path that began with the Knucklehead.

Keiffer also remembered that at that point it was a traditional engineering project—proceeding with too little regard for the concerns of manufacturing, the people who actually had to build the engine. Dick Click, the other technical manager at Capitol Drive, called Keiffer in August 1992. "Here we go again," Click sighed. Keiffer suggested getting a meeting together about the program.

Click and Keiffer attended the meeting, as did Dennert, Leroy Zindars, and Bruce Wells, the man who had birthed the Evo on the assembly line. Zindars and Wells represented manufacturing. For forty-five minutes, remembered Keiffer, "We bitched about 'what *they* were doing to us.'" And then a new thought came up. "Why don't the five of us take the program over and make sure they don't do it to us," Keiffer said. "We appointed ourselves to be the program board—five people who were going to do whatever it took to make this a success. It allowed us to cross the functional lines between departments."

The plan made sense to Dennert: "We became the tactical managers for the project, because we had all the people who were going to do the job."

Harley stylists once again tapped into their bin of classic parts to develop the FLSTN Softail Deluxe for 2005. Chrome and bright colors highlight this classic model.

ABOVE: Improved electronics highlight most of the new millennial models, and for 2001 this meant an improved, more powerful stereo sound system for the Road Glide.

RIGHT: Among the options for 2003 were the one-year-only Anniversary Edition paint jobs, in either silver or black, as shown on this Dyna Wide Glide.

The group of five went to Harley management and asked permission; they were more than a little surprised when the answer came back, "Cool. Go ahead." Shortly thereafter, the group went back to management, asking whom it wanted in overall charge of the program. Again, a shock: "Who do you want to run it?" was the reply. After some conferring, the five chose Keiffer.

Keiffer, tall and closely bearded, looks back to that period with some amazement, recalling his trepidation. There was a history of ambitious projects within Harley that came to dark ends and not-so-ambitious programs that ran years behind schedule. He remembered discussing the Classic Engine Project with Harley's upper management: "Every executive I talked to had a different idea about what they wanted from it. I was convinced that we could do it, but we had to nail down the scope. I had to get a mandate from the executives."

So during those days of 1992, the definition of the new engine was top priority. According to Dennert, "We had put together a list of features of what this engine could have, hundreds of features. A lot of these—twin-overhead-cam, multicylinder—got dropped. During 1992, we sorted through this entire list of items for manufacturability and reliability."

Dennert said some of the items were pretty simple: "Some of the criteria for a good engine were things like any single cover should be held on with bolts of one length, so a mechanic wouldn't have to worry about which bolt went where." Other things were done for noise reasons, such as setting the criteria "that covers can't carry any bushings or bearings," because those transmit mechanical noise to the cover.

"During 1992, we had active projects going on, testing ideas that might go into a new engine," Dennert explained. "There were a number of enabling technologies we were running, such as the straight crankpin and modified Evos with a single chain-driven cam. We presented styling with sketches of the single cam and various twin cams with different pushrod configurations. Styling liked the twin-cam concept. We actually built a twin cam in 1992 with gear-driven cams. We found that the chain-driven single cam gave us the best noise reduction, but the twin-cam was the most pleasing visually. So we combined the two."

The definition phase accelerated in mid-December, as Harley hired Bob Kobylarz from Kohler to be head of powertrain engineering. Keiffer remembered the strangeness of the situation: "It was my project and *his* engine." But the two quickly sorted out responsibilities. Keiffer would run the program and make sure it was on budget, on time, and had the resources required, while Kobylarz's group would be responsible for the design and engineering of the engine. With a top-level product planning review coming up at Keiffer's request in January, Kobylarz took his top engineers off-site for a week and narrowed down the choices.

"We came up with three options," Dennert remembered. "One was a minor upgrade to the Evo. The second was a significant change, but not as far as option three. Option three had a one-piece crank and automotive rods." The second option included both a new oiling system and the twin cams, while the first did not. Each of the three came with a complete list of features and an estimate on how long it would take to get each version into production.

In January 1993, those were the options presented to Harley's product planning committee, a select group of top executives and department heads who had to give the thumbs up or down on any major new program. The presenters made their pitch, and

"SOME OF THE CRITERIA FOR A GOOD ENGINE WERE THINGS LIKE ANY SINGLE COVER SHOULD BE ON WITH BOLTS OF ONE LENGTH, SO A MECHANIC WOULDN'T HAVE TO WORRY ABOUT WHICH BOLT WENT WHERE."

then were asked to wait outside. Keiffer remembers the wait being an hour, while Dennert is sure it was just fifteen minutes. In either case, it seemed forever. Finally the planning committee called them back in to say it had chosen option two: an all-new bottom end, carrying a largely carryover Evo top end. "At that time," Keiffer said, "it did not include revised displacement or the revised rear interface [the new gearbox mounting]."

But the best part was the commitment that had been won from Harley-Davidson CEO Jeff Bleustein: "This is it. We won't alter the scope of the program unless you ask for it." This was one program that wouldn't grow out of control as executives piled on features midstream.

"That was day one," Keiffer said, "of the P-22 project," the name he gave to the engine that would eventually become the Twin Cam, and the only name by which anyone within Harley-Davidson would use for the next five years. What did it mean? "Guys would guess," Keiffer said, "two cams and two cylinders, or something like that." Keiffer smiled and shook his head. They didn't have a clue, his body language was saying.

"It was after Catch-22. You know, 'Anyone sane enough to ask for a psychological discharge from World War II bomber duty was obviously not crazy enough to get it,' or something to that effect. This was Project-22, and it had its own catch: the only way for this project to be successful is if we understand the depth of our failures to this time."

And on that cheery note, Keiffer and the others set Harley-Davidson on the road to the Twin Cam 88.

Softail enthusiasts have considered the sleek FXSTD Deuce as one of the cleanest styling jobs Harley has ever produced. This 2003 is a fine example of that.

"The plan we had brought to the product planning committee estimated we could build the first running engine in ten months. December 3 was the day," Bruce Dennert recalled, the man who led the engine mechanical design group. "The first engine ran on December 2."

"What made that possible was the preliminary decision making that had emerged in the past year. "We had a nice definition of what we wanted to do; we didn't have to try something and show it," says Bruce Leppanen, design lead for the P-22's bottom end. The bottom end was where all the action was; initially the idea had been that the top end would only be lightly modified Evo components. "Forty-five-degree, air-cooled, in-line cylinders; vertically split crankcase; twin cam with chain drive—those had all been decided," Leppanen said, who had earlier been the lead engine designer on the five-speed Sportster. "Then we gave ourselves a lot of soft definitions: commonized fasteners, no leaks, easy to work on without a lot of specialty tools, easy to assemble."

"We started with a crank and deck height and cylinder-angle and cam positions, and started piecing it together," Leppanen remembered. "We had done some previous work with Jeff Coughlin on a straight crankpin," so that was incorporated. Once basic locations were nailed down, the next question presented itself: what do you do for an oil pump? Leppanen answered that: "We had a lot of options. Internal oil pump, gerotor type, on the crankshaft made more sense. Once that decision was made, making the models and designs of the oil pump was just a task." Leppanen is similarly nonchalant about

This 2003 Dyna Wide Glide sports the silver-and-black Anniversary Edition paint job.

Harley began its CVO program with the last editions of the Evolution engine, but the CVO division really hit its stride with the Twin Cam models. *Kevin Wing*

the design of the cams and their drives. Once using twin cams had been decided, he considers that the rest was just detail design and execution.

None of these design decisions took place in a vacuum; the very air around Harley engineering percolated with ideas that had yet to find a home in a production engine. Bruce Dennert, in a Saturday morning bull session at Zorba's, had proposed an internal oil pump for the new Big Twin, with a cam-carrying spider plate serving to route oil, eliminating numerous drilled passages from cases or covers that were truly manufacturing headaches. And gerotor pumps driven directly by the crank weren't new ideas at Harley either; the first VR-1000 layouts back in 1988 had proposed such a design, which eliminated a shaft, a gear pair, and the associated bearings, and thus reduced both cost and noise—a particular concern with Harley engineering. Only the reality of 50-degree lean angles in road racing and the need for ground clearance had prevented the VR from having a similar pump sticking off the end of its crank.

"The engine size wasn't fast and hard," Leppanen said. "Bruce Dennert's performance prediction programs helped develop the size we needed."

Dennert remembered, "We changed to 1,450 very early in the year as we were doing the vehicle performance predictions. We started the design road at 1,350 with the option of 1,450, perhaps eventually going to 1,550. We quickly changed that when marketing wanted a clear improvement in performance over the Evo." The actual bore and stroke were

The Road King Classic
combined the style of a
bespoke custom bike with
the functionality of a factory
tourer. *Kevin Wing*

Although the Road King Classic had once been one of Harley's most popular models, its popularity waned in the twenty-first century and it eventually disappeared from the lineup. *Kevin Wing*

THE PARTS THAT WOULD CHANGE THE LEAST DURING P-22 DEVELOPMENT WERE THE CRANKCASES AND THE FLYWHEELS, THE TWO PARTS THAT HAD BEEN MOST THOROUGHLY STUDIED EARLY ON.

chosen so that the shaking force, and thus vibration, "would be no greater than a 1,340, which meant bigger on bore and down on stroke," Dennert said. So by early 1993, the P-22 was nailed down as a 1,450, with the 1,550cc option available for later production or for parts or accessories kits.

"Part of the engine definition," recalled Leppanen, "was that you have to prepare it for upgrades. The idea was you shouldn't have to buy a crankcase to build a hot rod. We made a lot of the bearings oversized. Even the cylinder stud spacing took this into account. We asked, 'How big can you go out on the stud pattern and still get the head gasket to seal?' We built a lot of growth potential into the engine. Even the cam lifter was designed to work with high-performance cams without modifications."

A lot of the bottom-end strength was simply in the detail design of the crankcases. By then the problems with Evo cases—which in hot-rodded engines would crack in predictable locations—were very well understood. Skip Metz talks about the testing that had been done: "Under a high-speed camera, you could really see Evo cases moving around; it almost looked like breathing. We knew where the weak spots were." Leppanen filled those in with good basic engineering design practices, doing the obvious like "putting all the load bearing walls in line, and not putting notches in them." He then passed his CAD models to Harley's analytical engineering group. There the engineers used computerized finite element analysis (FEA) to predict stresses long before a casting was made, and Leppanen refined his design based on those predictions.

Dennert noted that Harley went so far as to buy a prototype die to get the high-pressure die-casting process down. "That development die cost a quarter-million dollars

The year 2003 marked the end of the road for the regular production Heritage Softail Springer. *Kevin Wing*

and was intended to be thrown away," Dennert said. But it allowed the actual crankcase design made with the actual production process to be tested early in the program. "There were lab tests," Metz said, "of loading and cycling of the first prototypes to see if they duplicated what the FEA models predicted before they were ever put into an engine."

The testing paid off. The parts that would change the least during P-22 development were the crankcases and the flywheels, the two parts that had been most thoroughly studied early on. According to Metz, the only serious problem ever to show up on the crankcases was with some cracking on the front left motor mount, a problem that quickly yielded to a slight increase in the fillet on the mount.

According to Dennert, "The design team was really rocking and rolling in 1993. No one was going to stand in the way of that engine running in December. By August, all major pieces and patterns were being made. For the cylinder heads, we used old Evo tooling and modified that."

If you could look back at the engine that came together for the December 2 run, it would have been recognizably a Twin Cam 88. The bore and stroke were 3.75 inches by 4.00 inches, the same as the production engine. The cams were in their current locations, driven by similar chains. The gerotor oil pump was there. The crankcases were identical to the 1999 production cases in all details except the passages connecting cam case to crankcase. Visually, though, the top end looked like an Evo, with the same finning, and the various covers were clearly prototypes, not the final styled pieces. And there were all the hoses and instrumentation wires attached that clearly identified the engine as an engineering prototype.

All 2003 models were available with a black paint scheme that celebrated the Motor Company's 100th anniversary. *Kevin Wing*

Although touring models usually comprise the meat of Harley's Screamin' Eagle-CVO offerings, the company occasionally offered a Softail or Dyna model. *Kevin Wing*

But it fired up on December 2, 1993, and boy, did it run. According to Dennert, "Fortunately or unfortunately, that first engine ran for 300 hours on life support"—referring to the huge external scavenge pump that vacuumed the bottom end of the prototype. "We thought it was going to be a cakewalk . . . and then the later engines went to hell. It was a long time before we got another that lasted as well as the first one."

As soon as engines were run without life support, it was clear that the first attempt at an oiling system wasn't going to be the last. The problems took years to solve and delayed the release of the engine. Before the difficulties were over, the weary P-22 program leaders began joking about digging up and reviving Bill Harley, the designer of the Knucklehead, and getting his advice on how to do an oiling system.

The actual solutions came from a young engineer named Paul Troxler, brought in from the outside to specifically solve the oil system problems. According the Skip Metz, Harley first went to the Southwest Research Institute, a well-respected engineering consultancy, simply to help the Motor Company on testing. "We didn't have enough dyno capacity," Metz said, "and we went down to see if they could run our engines. We eventually signed a contract and started to send our engines there."

After that, it was a small step to a second contract with Southwest to specifically look at the P-22's oiling and breathing system. "We needed someone," Metz said, "who could sort out the technical issues. We were working with Dr. Ping Sui to do a computer model of flow. Paul Troxler was a design engineer at Southwest and was assigned to work with Dr. Sui on this project.

Orange-and-black paint schemes have always been integral to Harley's CVO models. *Kevin Wing*

"Paul is a very analytical engineer. He's the kind of guy in a college engineering class you always wanted to strangle, ten pages ahead of the instructor. We hired him away from Southwest to understand how the test engine related to Dr. Sui's model. He spent his next two years on the motoring dyno, and if it hadn't been for him, we'd still be in trouble."

The problem with the P-22 oiling system was easy to explain: oil was where it shouldn't be, most specifically coming out on the breather and oozing from gasketed joints. According to Troxler, "The general layout of what you see today was in the original oil system design. There are subtle differences but not major differences. Initially there was an attempt to drain the cam case into the crankcase and have a single scavenge pickup. But the velocity of the air coming into the cam case, through ports in the crankcase wall, was keeping the oil from draining. The scavenge system was the problem."

The beginning of the solution was to abandon the single oil pickup and go to a "split-kidney" dual-passage scavenge, as had recently been tried for the Sportster. The separate scavenge paths for the crankcase were still connected by a high port, and there were still high levels of oil carryover in the crankcase. The excessive oil from the crankcase would come in the cam case through that port as mist and then get carried up through the breather. No P-22 would never see production until it kept its oil inside the engine. Troxler essentially moved into the one test cell on Juneau that was set up with a motoring dyno, one that used an electric motor to spin a noncombusting P-22. The engines were fitted with Plexiglas covers and windows to allow direct observation of oil flow.

"It was long days, and weekends, and Saturdays," Troxler said. "Often I would have the test cell running two shifts a day. I'd have two engines. One would run shifts one and two while the other engine was being reconfigured. The third shift would swap engines. That scenario went on two months straight while we were working on the crankcase scavenge pump. Everybody and their brother had an idea, and we tried just about every one of them."

Another engineer, Mark Hoffman, thought that reducing the velocity of air in the pushrod tubes—which provided the breathing path between cam case and cylinder head—would give the oil more time to settle back and thus reduce carryover. It did, but the big pushrod tubes that were required weren't an acceptable solution to styling.

Troxler had saved his personal idea for last—totally sealing the crankcase from the cam case. Eliminate the passages between the two chambers, and "lo, and behold," Troxler said, "the carryover dropped." With that change, and with the addition of both a coalescing air/oil separator and a tortuous path separator in the cylinder head, the test bikes at Talladega no longer generated oil carryover unless the engine had other problems.

But the oil system gremlins weren't finished. With the crankcase newly sealed, less oil made it up from the cam case to the cylinder heads and the breather, but crankcase scavenging actually worsened. Oil would build up excessively in the crankcase at 1,500 to 2,500 rpm, just the type of speed Big Twins are frequently run. The solution to that took months and was almost bizarre. "The fix was to restrict the inlet to the scavenge line," Troxler said. The scavenge passage was a longish $7/16$-inch line connecting crankcase to oil pump. "It was an acoustic phenomenon," Troxler said. "The passage was pressurizing when the piston came back down, filling the air, and—when the passage was depressurizing with the crankcase—the air was coming back out, preventing oil from coming into the passage. We found it out experimentally, and only then modeled it on the computer to show how the restriction worked."

Of course, anyone looking at a Twin Cam crankcase is going to wonder why there's a roughly $3/16$-inch hole leading to a $7/16$-inch passage. "Yeah," Troxler said, "and they're going to assume more is better and drill this passage out, and boy, are they going to be sorry."

The Road King models are touring bikes that look like custom cruisers. *Kevin Wing*

THE RESULTS WERE STAGGERING; WHILE OTHER CHANGES TO THE ENGINE WERE CUTTING A DEGREE HERE, TWO DEGREES THERE, SHUTTING DOWN THE OIL FLOW TO THE CYLINDER HEAD AND THE ROCKER SHAFTS DROPPED OIL TEMPERATURES BY 30 TO 35 DEGREES.

The more than two years spent chasing down the oil system issues as well as other problems guaranteed that the P-22 would miss its original 1997 model year production target by at least a year. To some extent, Harley, which had not done an all-new engine in decades, didn't know what it was getting into when it started the project. But it quickly sought out the expertise it needed, and added new skills and abilities along with new personnel to its engineering staff.

When Troxler looks back, he said, "Much of what was done with the scavenge and breather system was done by blacksmithing and the traditional approach of just getting in and trying things. Someday, new tools of computational fluid dynamics will speed up development. I'm trying new tools now, using the Twin Cam 88 for my test case."

Bob Kobylarz, former head of engine engineering, summed it up: "We're not intimidated by oil systems on Big Twins anymore. We didn't understand how it worked; now we do."

By 1996, test bikes were running with prototype Twin Cam engines, Harley's dynos were fully occupied with Twin Cams hammering away, and the development was in full flurry. But not all was going well, and the problems went beyond the oil system difficulties that had already pushed the release of the engine a year beyond its original 1997 schedule.

The most reliable Harley-Davidson engine ever: that was the goal for the Twin Cam 88. Early testing, though, revealed some obstacles to achieving that goal. With the increased displacement and power, the Twin Cam generated more heat than the Evo, and that heat was translating into higher piston temperatures.

That was a problem for aluminum pistons. In almost every way, aluminum serves well in pistons. It's strong, with a strength-to-weight ratio similar to steel. It's castable, so complex piston shapes can be molded, rather than expensively machined. It conducts heat exceptionally well, so combustion heat can be pulled from the piston crown to the cylinder walls, preventing hot spots. Unfortunately, though, aluminum quickly gets weak in the knees as temperatures rise past 400 degrees. According to Nicolae Glaja, the Romanian-born development engineer who was involved with many of the temperature control issues on the P-22, "We had to drop the piston temperature to ensure that there would be no degradation all the way to 100,000 miles."

The chosen approach was one found on many diesels, and many high-performance, imported motorcycle engines: oil jets spraying up from the crankcase on the bottom of the piston crowns. Once the oil system and the crankcases were modified to include the jets, they did exactly what they were supposed to do: they pulled the piston temperatures down to acceptable levels. But there was a not entirely unexpected cost: heat from the pistons was pulled into the engine oil, and now oil temperatures were too high.

"In early 1996," said Skip Metz, engineering project leader for the P-22 program, "we got permission from the Styling Department to start working on an oil cooling system. We came up with a nice oil cooler that mounted down low on the chassis." The oil cooler, according to those who saw it, was a particularly attractive unit, much nicer than most aftermarket versions, and it dropped oil temperatures to acceptable levels. But within the company it brought up bad memories of pre-Evo engines that ran too hot and the oil coolers that had been affixed to them. It wasn't a particularly elegant solution.

But time was running short. According to Metz, "In late 1996, we were running the QRL (quality reliability longevity) test on bikes fitted with the oil cooler at the VW Volvo

ABOVE: The Heritage Classic Softail models are custom cruisers that function as touring motorcycles. *Kevin Wing*

LEFT: The Heritage Softail Classic is one of Harley's longest-running motorcycle models. *Kevin Wing*

For 2003 Harley produced a Screamin' Eagle version of its popular Road King touring model. *Kevin Wing*

proving grounds near Phoenix. [Passing this test was essential for production approval for the 1998 model year.] The results were pretty good, and the durability was pretty good. We still had some problems with noisy cam drives and that side of the engine. There were about five specific problems we identified on that test that we didn't like, but we thought we could address those problems in time for 1998. But we came to a roadblock. Styling said there was no way they could see an oil cooler on this engine. Oil coolers were seen as a Band-Aid for the basic design of the engine."

The members of the QRL committee soon were meeting with the members of the product planning committee, reviewing the oil cooler issue and the decision for 1998 production. "Their consensus," Metz said of a December 16, 1996, meeting, "was that the oil cooler was a bad thing and that we couldn't go into production with it." The P-22 program had just crashed into a wall over the oil cooler; a very significant redesign of the engine would be required to dispense with it.

Production in 1998 was history. To make the 1999 model year, "we had from Christmas to April 1, 1997, to solve the problem," Metz said. "That four-month period was the roughest period of the whole program."

Doug Grant, an engineer from the applied mechanics group at Harley, had been assigned to track and fix engine leaks and seeps. He was reassigned to help develop a mathematical model of the engine that predicted heat flows and temperatures. The thermal model showed that increased finning, as everyone suspected, would help. The Twin Cam, at that time, still had Evo-sized fins. But the big-fin concept had to be proven before a million dollars of already-ordered production tooling was scrapped.

Harley engineering began running on war mode in the winter of 1997. "One of the things that really helped us during this period was working with Jim Feuling," Metz

remembered. "Earl Werner [Harley engineering chief] had known Jim from his past life at GM [General Motors], and thought he could help us. Jim has a list of patents as long as your arm on things he has done on engines, many things that aren't obvious. He had a lot of ideas we tried. Some of them worked and some of them didn't—but he got us to open up our minds and not to think we couldn't do something in a specific length of time. You can have a conversation with him, and he'll have something fabricated and running on a dyno in a couple of days."

During that period, parts were being developed and tested before they were ever designed. "We contacted Volvo to see if we could use their test track near Phoenix, and set up shop in their development lab for four to six weeks in March and April of 1997," Metz recalled. "We had motorcycles and engines at Jim's place in Ventura, California, and used his facility as a resource for prototypes. We'd fly parts over to the Phoenix airport and test them for a day or two. We were working from sketches and phone calls and just trying things, new oil pan baffles, finning, etc. Volvo's 2-mile test track was right next to its lab, and we could go do parade laps or high-speed laps. It was a little skunkworks, to look at oil temperatures and get things done without the usual bureaucracy."

Development Engineer Glaja was in Phoenix, and he remembered how hard the battle was. "To shave 10 degrees Fahrenheit out of the oil is a big thing; you have to fight for each degree." Big, welded-on fins were helping, as was oil flow changes in the oil tank that increased cooling, as was Feuling's patented exhaust valve and exhaust port, but those changes in and of themselves didn't add to the kind of drop in oil temperatures required to get rid of the cooler.

The big win would come from an insight from Milwaukee. Ben Vandenhoven took time from his work on the counterbalanced Twin Cam Beta engine and went down to a dyno

While all Screamin' Eagles featured custom parts up the wazoo, the most obvious distinguishing features were their striking paint schemes. This 2003 Screamin' Eagle Road King features Centennial Gold livery with Vivid Black and Burgundy accents. *Kevin Wing*

By 2016 the base prices of some of Harley's CVO touring models started on the north side of $40,000. *Kevin Wing*

cell and began a test program that restricted oil flow to various parts of the engine. The objective was to find out exactly where the engine oil was picking up most of its heat. The results were staggering; while other changes to the engine were cutting a degree here, two degrees there, shutting down the oil flow to the cylinder head and the rocker shafts dropped oil temperatures by 30 to 35 degrees.

"We were trying to cool the cylinder heads with excess oil flow," recollected Bruce Dennert, the man who led the initial mechanical design of the Twin Cam, "without doing a very good job." The situation was this: the biggest heat flow from the cylinder heads was to the atmosphere through the finning. The Twin Cam had been designed with heavy oil flow to the heads, far in excess of mechanical needs, with the undeveloped idea that it might help cooling. However, so much heat flowed through the heads that even the heavy oil flow couldn't significantly drop cylinder head temperatures. Yet, at the same time, the amount of heat picked up by the oil in the heads was huge from the point of view of the oil system, which was dealing with much smaller heat flows overall than the heads. "We rebalanced the oil flow," Dennert said, "and cut the oil flow to the heads to one-quarter to one-sixth of what we had previously. That was adequate for lubrication."

"Oil temperatures of 260 and 280 degrees were pretty common before the oil flow change," Metz said, "and that's pretty close to where oil starts to oxidize. Our target oil temperature was 230, and on the dyno, the [temperature-controlled] oil coolers were on more than they were off. After the oil flow change, the oil cooler never came on and the oil temperature was pretty much in the 215- and 220-degree range."

Except for its lack of ground clearance, Harley's modern Softail chassis proved surprisingly sporting, thanks to the rigidity the solid-mounted engine added to the chassis. *Kevin Wing*

So by the end of April 1997, solutions to the temperature problem were known. The problem was to get them incorporated into design-intent bikes by August to allow sufficient time for testing for 1999 production. Brian Thate, senior project designer, was given the task of turning the concepts into production-ready designs. "Nick [Glaja] and Feuling took existing heads and welded on pieces near the exhaust ports. Then they gave the pieces to Willie G. and the styling guys. We had to take the final welded-up parts and get them into production," he said. "You couldn't do conventional drawings—there wasn't time. We made tooling off the 3-D models. Harley had guys flying over to Germany [where the tooling vendor was located] with SLA [stereo lithography, essentially a 3-D plastic printing technique from a CAD file] models to set tooling. We had design-intent cylinders and heads by August, but there were a lot of sleepless nights."

Of course, the big fins of the Twin Cam have since become its visual trademark. But they wouldn't have happened if the oil temperature problems hadn't reared their heads. Because the P-22 program started as a bottom-end redesign. styling had been told early on that it couldn't change the Evo finning. And by the time the problems emerged, engineering had assumed that styling was married to the look of the Evo-style top end. In the meantime, no one in upper management was volunteering the millions of dollars that it eventually took to give the Twin Cam its big fins. But the oil temperature problem broke the log jam, and while it delayed the Twin Cam a year, it's hard to do anything but applaud the big-finned, cool-running, macho-appearing final result.

The rubber-mounted Twin Cams entered production with the 1999 model year, to be followed a year later by the solidly mounted counterbalanced beta version of the new engine in the new Softails. While minor problems cropped up in cam bearings and cam sprocket retention, the new engine was all Harley could have asked for, offering vastly improved performance and reliability, and leading to new sales records.

CHAPTER 9

HARLEY-DAVIDSON IN THE TWENTY-FIRST CENTURY

BY STEVE ANDERSON

HARLEY HAD A KICKASS FIRST CENTURY. IT RODE THE FIRST MOTORCYCLE BOOM, SURVIVED THE MODEL T, DEFINED THE AMERICAN MOTORCYCLE WITH ITS KNUCKLEHEAD, BECAME PART OF A HUGE CONGLOMERATE, PRODUCED TENS OF THOUSANDS OF MACHINES OF QUESTIONABLE QUALITY IN THE SEVENTIES, ESCAPED THE HUGE CONGLOMERATE AND TEETERED ON EXTINCTION IN THE EARLY EIGHTIES, DESIGNED AND INTRODUCED MUCH-IMPROVED-YET-STILL-CLASSIC PRODUCTS, AND WENT ON TO ALMOST UNIMAGINABLE SUCCESS GOING INTO ITS HUNDREDTH BIRTHDAY. BUT WHAT ABOUT ITS SECOND CENTURY? WHAT WILL HARLEY IN THE TWENTY-FIRST CENTURY LOOK LIKE? THE FIRST HINT OF THAT CAME WITH THE MOTOR COMPANY'S FIRST NEW CENTURY PROJECT: THE V-ROD.

THE V-ROD

The 2002 V-Rod broke away from Harley's Big Twin heritage. A Porsche-designed engine—an engine with twin cams instead of pushrods, four valves in each cylinder, fuel injection, and water cooling—powered the aluminum-skinned bike. It redlined at 9,000 rpm and easily pumped 115 horsepower or more at the crankshaft. It was not your father's Harley.

But the V-Rod, regardless of its innovations, was still solidly rooted in Harley's past—its recent past, that is. As Harley-Davidson powertrain engineer Joe Schafter noted of the V-Rod's Revolution engine, "We kept the VR's [the VR1000, Harley's Superbike racer] architecture." Both the Revolution and the racing-only VR (a project started in the late

eighties) share some basic features not found on other Harley engines. Start with the 60-degree V-angle, 15 degrees wider than that of Harley's air-cooled engines.

At the VR's introduction, Jeff Coughlin, Harley's project leader for the V-Rod, commented on even more similarities between the two: "The balance shaft of the VR has stayed, and in relatively that same position." A twenty-first-century motorcycle can't vibrate annoyingly—with the rapid acceptance of the counterbalanced Softails, Harley customers had already signaled that they were ready for the low-vibration future.

In a trend that will shape every Harley-Davidson engine design forever on, the quest for mechanical noise reduction was the most compelling reason for Harley to have a new design for the Revolution. Noise laws worldwide have been getting stricter. As a twenty-first-century engine, the Revolution had to make meeting twenty-first-century regulations easier.

The need for a new design around a known architecture drove the second important aspect of the V-Rod project: the hiring of Porsche to handle the details. "We were pretty busy with the Twin Cam when this project started," said Coughlin—so busy that an engineering shortage prevented Harley from doing the engine in-house. Porsche Engineering Services, the car company's consulting division, had worked closely with Harley before, including designing the never-produced V-Four Nova in the last days of AMF ownership. The project started when Erik Buell recruited Porsche to do the first water-cooled performance engine for Buell, based on the VR, but that project turned into a joint Buell/Harley program, and then as the initial engine concept was reshaped by Harley-Davidson styling group to a bulkier concept, to a Harley-only project. The Germans and just a small team of Milwaukee engineers would transform the VR concept into a new engine. The emphasis would be on strength, produceability, and quiet running, rather than the performance-at-any-cost or at-any-noise-level goals of the VR.

Harley's 2002 VRSCA V-Rod, a model unlike any other bike from Milwaukee, ever. The V-twin engine has dual overhead camshafts, four valves per cylinder, and liquid cooling.

A TWENTY-FIRST-CENTURY MOTORCYCLE CAN'T VIBRATE ANNOYINGLY—WITH THE RAPID ACCEPTANCE OF THE COUNTERBALANCED SOFTAILS, HARLEY CUSTOMERS HAD ALREADY SIGNALED THAT THEY WERE READY FOR THE LOW-VIBRATION FUTURE.

It's not hard to find Porsche's influence inside the Revolution. The five-speed gearbox comes from German supplier Gertag (manufacturer of BMW motorcycle gear sets). As in most Porsche engines, the Revolution's connecting rods are forged in one piece with end caps cracked away after the big end is machined for perfect alignment.

But if the V-Rod's engine was a joint project, the rest of the machine was all Milwaukee, the manifestation of a vision of Willie G. Davidson and his colleagues in Harley's Styling Department. They began playing with a racing VR engine years ago, trying out such things as building a VR-powered Softail—or "learning what not to do," in Willie G.'s words. The proportions of a modern racing engine like the VR are completely different from classic Harley powerplants. The shrink-wrapped cases and small primary drives and gearboxes of modern engines have none of the visual mass of a Big Twin, and one simply can't take the place of the other. So Willie G. and company began looking for a different type of vehicle to house the engine.

The idea of a drag-racing-influenced machine was a natural. It fit with the high-performance goals of the new engine, and it fit with Willie's vision. Motorcycle drag racers had long swingarms to minimize wheelies; a long swingarm would look right coupled to the Revolution's short gearbox. They were long and low, and Willie liked that look. He also wanted the raked-out front ends that drag racers traditionally had. But that part of the vision initially ran into engineering resistance. "They told us it wouldn't work," he said. "And styling told engineering, 'You can't say no until you've tried it.'" So soon after, a Sportster test bike was given a new 34-degree steering head, with the forks kicked out another 4 degrees via offset triple clamps—a trick that Harley has been using for years on the FLs. That test Sportster handled well enough, so the V-Rod was granted its signature raked-out look.

On other parts of the machine, the stylists gave ground from the beginning. On Big Twins and Sportsters, they had for decades insisted on tiny, traditional mufflers—the shortie duals of a Big Twin have less than a liter of volume apiece and simply can't be quiet and non-restrictive at the same time. For the V-Rod, the mufflers and airbox would have to be huge to achieve the expected stock performance. Harley styling director Louie Netz says, "We knew we could solve the exhaust system—we knew we could make it a part of the look. The air cleaner, though—well, we knew we weren't going to hang it from the side. We'd already seem that on Buells." That left only one place for the airbox to go, above the engine in the normal gas tank location. The gas tank would have to go under the seat, which in turn dictated twin shocks—there was no room for both gasoline and a single shock in front of the back tire.

Willie G. and company also had a clear picture of what they wanted the V-Rod's frame to look like—they wanted it to literally frame the engine, like a picture frame, and "to hang the engine in space." Unlike most other Harleys—other than the FXRs—the V-Rod frame would be prominent on the outside of the bike, so it was vital it should look good. From the engineering point of view, it was equally vital that it be stiff for good handling. With these needs, styling and engineering began an iterative collaboration that ended with the design of the V-Rod frame you see today. Big tubes were good, because they could give adequate strength with ungussetted joints—a clean look that scored high with styling. The big tubes scored high with engineering for stiffness. Manufacturing processes were stressed to the limit for strength and appearance. All the joints are robotically welded to produce crisp, well-finished welds. The top frame tubes swoop in complex

curves that couldn't have been made at all a few years ago; now they're produced by hydroforming the tubes in hard dies that are capable of producing the three-dimensional shapes agreed upon by stylists and engineers.

Similarly, both engineers and stylists sweated the details on the radiator and oil coolers. There was no way that Willie G. was going to let the V-Rod ship with some black-painted boxy radiator on it, like some Japanese and European bikes. "It had to be an integral part of the design," he said. "Black paint doesn't make the radiator invisible." The solution emerged when both engineers and stylists were working together doing wind tunnel testing. It became clear that the space immediately behind the front tire was dead to airflow, and you might as well block the front of the radiator there. The next logical step was to make side scoops that caught clean air and directed it into the radiator. When those scoops were made of the same signature aluminum that covers the rest of the bike, Willie had the shape of his styling-integrated cooling system.

That aluminum was, in and of itself, another internal battle inside Harley-Davidson. No one doubted it was cool, and the engineers had no problems with the strong and light material. Instead, manufacturing questioned whether the aluminum parts could be produced at a reasonable price. The fenders, airbox cover, and radiator shrouds would all be anodized aluminum protected by only a thin clear coat. Anyone who has spent any time around a factory might question how such parts could make it through the manufacturing and assembly process without scratches, and how closely the color match could be held from one batch to another. As manufacturing experimented and hesitated to commit—after all, they would have to build it—Willie G. bombarded the manager of

Even though the 2004 VRSCB V-Rod retained the same aluminum dish wheels and other mechanical components found on the VRSCA, its black paint gave it a menacing appearance.

From the initial V-Rod, Harley developed a complete line of motorcycles. *Kevin Wing*

the Kansas City plant with e-mails, each containing a single word: aluminum. Whether it was this barrage or the completion of trials and experiments, manufacturing conceded: the first V-Rods would gleam in the metal just like a thirties DC-3, and look just as ready to take wing.

When that initial V-Rod l was seen in the metal, the first impressions were of gleaming silver, and of its size: it was long and very low. You could sit on it with your feet flat on the ground. While the spec sheet told that the first V-Rod weighed in at over 600 pounds wet, that's not what your senses reported. The machine felt small, narrow, and light, more Sportster than Big Twin in weight. Credit that to a low center of gravity, to a bike that carried its engine low and put a featherweight airbox up high and its 24 pounds of gasoline well below the seat.

The traditional Harley round ignition key was fitted just below the right side of the seat. Turned to the "on" position, the switch woke red warning lights on the big speedometer dial, and the electronically controlled speedo, fuel gauge, and tach needles swept from zero to maximum and back again, just to let you know they were working. A push on the starter button almost instantly set the cold V-Rod idling at 1,500 rpm, with none of the clanking and drama of a Big Twin start, and none of the long, loping pauses. You could put your gloves on while the V-Rod was warming up with no suspicion that it would flame out. The engine was smooth too—there was just the faintest quiver that could be felt at the end of the bars.

Pull out on to the street, and the V-Rod felt light, almost nothing like a Sportster. First, the seat was lower, and you sat more down into the V-Rod than on top of it. Second, it was roomy, with the pegs and controls a comfortable stretch away, rivaling if not bettering Softails for legroom.

Running the V-Rod out to 5,000 rpm put it in the heart of a meaty midrange, with the revs climbing quickly. From there it was just a blink to the 9,000-rpm red line; it was all too easy to bang against the rev limiter, which momentarily killed the engine. But if you were attentive and clicked into second quickly, you were rewarded with a further forward lunge, and yet another through third. You could be at 100 miles per hour in just seconds, with the V-Rod still pulling hard. If you tucked in like Scottie Parker and held on tight, you would soon be rewarded with a top speed never before seen on a production Harley: 140 miles per hour.

What was truly exceptional was how smoothly, readily, and precisely the V-Rod gave you this performance. The injection provided seamless mixture control, so that power delivered exactly matched what your throttle hand requested. Vibration was almost—but not quite—nonexistent: there was just enough reaching you past the counterbalancer's efforts and through the rubber mounts to know that there was a V-twin powering this machine, and not an electric motor.

In handing, the V-Rod sets its own course. Its long wheelbase, long trail, and raked-out steering made for a machine that felt slightly ungainly at parking lot speeds, but fortunately its low seating position and low center of gravity kept rider confidence high. At any road speed, the V-Rod stabilized wonderfully, and its stout 48mm fork tubes ensured a solid connection between handlebars and tire. Turn the bars, and—particularly at 30 miles per hour or less—the V-Rod almost seemed to have power steering, falling into turns eagerly.

WHAT WAS TRULY EXCEPTIONAL WAS HOW SMOOTHLY, READILY, AND PRECISELY THE V-ROD GAVE YOU THIS PERFORMANCE.

The V-Rod's liquid-cooled Revolution engine was the most powerful in Harley's lineup at the time of its introduction.
Kevin Wing

ABOVE: In spite of its liquid-cooled engine, the V-Rod maintained the wasp-waisted profile that defines all Harley-Davidson motorcycles. *Kevin Wing*

RIGHT: While the V-Rod engine might trace its DNA back to the VR1000 Superbike racer of the nineties, its cruiser styling limited cornering clearance and kept it from being anyone's favorite track-day motorcycle. *Kevin Wing*

All in all, the first V-Rod was functionally and visually the winner that Harley was looking for and, in its first year, experienced to the all-too-usual waiting lists and dealer price gouging. But the V-Rod lacked in long-term sales legs. Over the years, it was improved, gaining a 240mm section rear tire, a more massive look, and a more powerful 1,250cc engine, but it never caught on as Harley desired. And the Revolution engine never was used in anything other the V-Rod family of power cruisers. While V-Rods were still in Harley's lineup in 2016, insiders reported that would be the last production year, as the upgrades required to meet future regulations simply weren't economic at the sales volumes achieved.

THE STREET 500 AND THE STREET 750

At the 2013 EICMA show in Milan, the Motor Company announced its first all-new model range since the V-Rod: the 2014 Street 500 and 750. The two shared a common engine design, the Revolution X. As its name indicated, the Revolution X shared characteristics with the V-Rod's Revolution engine: water cooling, a 60-degree V angle, and four valves per cylinder. As with the 883 and 1200 Sportster engines, the big and little Revolution X engines were different by only a few parts, as both share the same 66mm stroke.

The Street project was initiated during Keith Wandell's tenure as CEO at Harley, and the project had some unusual aspects. As with the V-Rod, the detail engine design was outsourced, but this time not to Porsche, but to AVL's division in India. In addition, many of the components of the two machines were sourced from India or elsewhere in Asia, and the two bikes were assembled in either Harley-Davidson's Bawal, India, facility for distribution worldwide, or the Kansas City plant that also builds Sportsters for distribution in the United States and Canada. In general, regardless of which plant the machines are assembled in, the components used are the same.

The Street 750 offered up 57 horsepower and had a wet weight of just over 500 pounds, much lighter and almost 10 horsepower more powerful than an 883 Sportster. But the most important figures were the prices: $6,700 for the 500, and $7,500 for the Street 750. It remains to be seen if these new machines will fare better than the V-Rod in the long term, but for now they are the least expensive path into the Harley brand.

PROJECT LIVEWIRE

The Motor Company showed off its electric bike prototype, Project Livewire, in June 2014. Mission Motors assisted with initial development, and thirty or so prototypes have been used for demonstration rides and as Scarlett Johansson's mount in the Avenger movies. Insiders claim that the intent was originally to put the machine into immediate production, but lingering technical issues and a very high price prevented that. In any case, the bike was built around a (unusually) longitudinally mounted permanent magnet AC motor that drove the rear wheel through a right angle gear set and a belt final drive. The frame was Harley's first all-aluminum structure. Battery capacity has never been stated but had to be significantly less than 10 kilowatt hour given the short, 50-miles-per-hour range claimed between rechargings. With the high torque of the electric powertrain from 0 rpm, no clutch or gearbox were fitted, and acceleration was brisk, with Harley claiming a 0-to-60 mile-per-hour acceleration time of four seconds. Work continues at Harley on electric motorcycles, but no timeframe for their release has been given.

BOTH ENGINEERS AND STYLISTS SWEATED THE DETAILS ON THE RADIATOR AND OIL COOLERS. THERE WAS NO WAY THAT WILLIE G. WAS GOING TO LET THE V-ROD SHIP WITH SOME BLACK-PAINTED BOXY RADIATOR ON IT, LIKE SOME JAPANESE AND EUROPEAN BIKES.

THE FUTURE: THE BIG TWIN

Harley-Davidson and the Big Twin are synonymous, and that will not change. The vast majority of the Motor Company's sales are Big Twins, and nothing is on the horizon to change that. Rumors emerging from Harley on future Big Twins point to more of the same, except more so. Tightening emission and noise laws point to improvements in cooling, with something like Harley's current Precision Cooling system adding some water cooling to what will remain a substantially air-cooled engine. Every effort will be to maintain and enhance its heritage appearance while improving performance and durability. Variable valve timing would allow more torque to be made over a broader band while enhancing emissions performance, so that is one technology you can almost certainly expect to see on the future Big Twin.

Also expect some surprises from the very energized and expanding Motor Company. Harley now has the resources to do both the traditional and the unexpected, so expect the electrified fruit of Project Live Wire even while some Big Twin models look even more like products that come from the 1930s or the 1940s, or perhaps there will even be a range topper custom that comes in above the Big Twin—anything is possible. The main thing is to expect Harley to continue to listen closely to its customers, to continue to have people who ride and love motorcycles plan the next products, to continue to give us motorcyclists the machines we want. And if it can continue to do that, the Motor Company should have as wild ride through the twenty-first century as it did in the twentieth.

In 2013 Harley-Davidson introduced two new middleweight motorcycles, the Street 500 and the Street 750, at the Milan motorcycle show. *Kevin Wing*

ABOVE: Like all modern Harleys, the Street 750 had a belt final drive. *Kevin Wing*

LEFT: The light weight of the Street 750 gave it nimble handling that made it an ideal bike for newer riders. *Kevin Wing*

CHAPTER 10
RACING

BY ALLAN GIRDLER

ONE WORD DEFINES HARLEY-DAVIDSON: *TRADITION*. RACING IS ONE OF HARLEY'S OLDEST TRADITIONS. FROM ITS EARLIEST YEARS, THE MOTOR COMPANY'S REPUTATION FOR QUALITY AND VALUE WAS LARGELY BASED ON SPORT AND COMPETITION. SINCE THE CURRENT AMA GRAND NATIONAL CHAMPIONSHIP BEGAN IN 1954, HARLEY RIDERS HAVE WON THE NO. 1 PLATE 38 TIMES IN 49 YEARS. THE MANUFACTURER'S TITLE RACE BEGAN IN 1972, AND H-D HAS WON IT ALL BUT EIGHT SEASONS. THAT'S A RECORD NO OTHER MAKER CAN MATCH.

Yet racing is something the folks who run the show have never really wanted to talk about. Pull into a gas station anywhere in the United States with a vintage track bike in your truck and someone is sure to exclaim, "A Harley? When did Harley get into racing?"

"About 1908" is the correct answer. In fact, Harleys were taking part in sports events before that.

There are reasons for the company's shyness about its racing successes that go back to the very beginning of the sport of motorcycling. Early Harley-Davidson ads mentioned almost in passing that Harley owners had won this race or that rally, noting that the factory hadn't spent any money or even helped in any way.

Then came 1908. Walter Davidson, a natural athlete, entered a stock—albeit carefully prepared—single-cylinder Model 4 in an enduro on New York's Long Island. Davidson didn't just win; he won with a perfect score. The feat collected headlines coast to coast. The next year, Davidson and his pals rode four stock machines in an endurance run from Cleveland to Indianapolis. They turned in a set of perfect scores and took home the team prize.

Impressive stuff, but the day came when reliability was no longer an issue, and road bikes didn't make the news. Indian and others now forgotten, like Merkel and Thor, fielded professional racing teams on purebred racers. Their racers earned acclaim, and prior to World War I, Indian topped the sales charts, worldwide.

Russell "Kid" Fischer on Knuth Special #4. In the 1920s, Milwaukee dealer Bill Knuth built professional Class A hillclimb machines for his shop-sponsored hillclimb team. The Knuth Special used full overhead valve technology when most guys still rode side-valve (flathead) machines.

BOARDS AND BAKED DIRT, 1914–1931

On July 4, 1914, at Dodge City, Kansas, Harley-Davidson fielded the firm's first factory team, six top stars of the day riding stripped and tuned versions of production street twins. Spectators watched four Harleys fail to finish the 300-mile race, and the two that finished were back behind the pack.

H-D hired an engineer with racing experience, and the team's results improved. In 1915, H-D fielded souped-up F-head machines and some overhead-valve racers with four valves per cylinder. This was the first of a series of golden ages. Back then, cities closed streets so motorcycles could race on real roads. They raced on fairgrounds ovals, usually half-mile or mile tracks used for horse racing, or they raced at speeds of 120 miles per

No motorcycle stands more for Class C flat-track racing than Harley's XR750. Its low-profile gas tank is an icon among American race bikes.

The silhouette of this 1922 JD board track racer illustrates that aerodynamics was as important during those early years as it is for racers now.

hour on fearsome banked ovals made of splintery boards. Racing was a popular form of entertainment before World War I, and motorcycle races drew huge crowds.

Harley-Davidson offered racing models for sale to private racers, further increasing the sport's popularity.

Perhaps "offered" should be clarified. In 1915, Excelsior advertised its Model 16-S.C., winner of the American National championship, as "the fastest motorcycle ever built." It came with a full-race 61-cubic-inch V-twin and sold for $250. In 1916, Indian advertised its Model H, a racer with a 61-cubic-inch V-twin overhead-valve engine, available with four valves per cylinder, priced at $350. The 1916 Harley catalog features the "Twin Cylinder model 17," with a 61-cubic-inch eight-valve engine, but with all the specifications vague or optional. The price was $1,500. The outrageous price guaranteed that no average racer would be able to purchase this exotic racing machine.

Instead, the factory assembled a pro team nicknamed "The Wrecking Crew." Harley built only enough bikes to fill the team's needs, plus a handful for selected dealers and tuners, including some from overseas.

The first 61s used shortened spindly frames and direct drive, had no brakes or suspension, and used tires no thicker than your thumb.

Harley's men in charge, Chief Engineer William Harley and Racing Engineer William Ottaway, knew enough to know they didn't know everything. When the new Harley engines didn't equal rival Indian's 61 twins, H-D hired English wizard Harry Ricardo and kept him under contract until the Harley 61 cranked out 55 horsepower. When Merkel went broke, Harley hired its best man, Maldwyn Jones, who arrived at the Motor Company with a machine he'd had Merkel build to his specs. The Harley shop fitted the bike with a Harley engine. Jones said the Merkel's forks worked better, so for several years, the Harley team used Merkel forks.

The racing was almost too good, in the sense that seeds were incredible. There were injuries and even deaths, including spectators struck by out-of-control machines, which led to the board tracks being sensationalized in the press as "Murder Domes." In 1921, Otto Walker won the Fresno board mile on a Harley 61 at an average speed on 101.4 miles per hour, making Walker the first motorcycle racer in the world to finish a race with an average speed faster than 100 miles per hour.

Just how fierce were the machines of this era? In 1922 the lap record for the first mile was 39.6 seconds. The modern record? Ricky Graham did one lap of the Springfield, Illinois, mile in 34.548 seconds. So in nearly eighty years, we've shortened the time for the mile by 5 seconds. Those old guys were fast.

In 1921, the Harley Wrecking Crew won all the national titles. The next year, the Harley factory pulled the plug on its racing team, and either sold or gave away the machines.

ABOVE: Irving Janke (left) won the race at Dodge City in 1916 aboard a Harley Eight-Valve.

BELOW: The compact F-head Model JD displaced 61 cubic inches. It was one of the fan favorites among dirt-track fans during the Roaring Twenties.

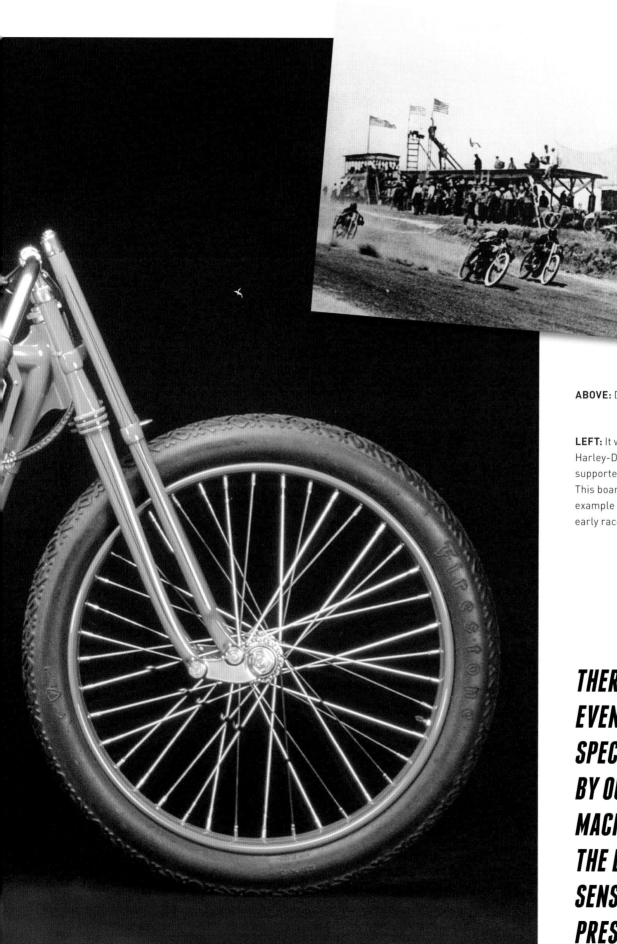

ABOVE: Dodge City race, 1916.

LEFT: It wasn't until 1914 that Harley-Davidson officially supported a factory race team. This board track racer is an example of how specialized those early racers were.

THERE WERE INJURIES AND EVEN DEATHS, INCLUDING SPECTATORS STRUCK BY OUT-OF-CONTROL MACHINES, WHICH LED TO THE BOARD TRACKS BEING SENSATIONALIZED IN THE PRESS AS "MURDER DOMES."

PRODUCTION RACING RETURNS: 1931–1935

The Great Depression nearly killed the sport of motorcycling. How salvation arrived is a story so unusual and improbable that it must be true, mostly because it's too unlikely to be believable fiction.

As racing evolved, the various sanctioning bodies developed three levels of competition. Class A allowed pure-race machines, with displacement the only limit. Class B was professional and required production-based engines modified for racing. Class C was for amateurs, typically owners who raced the machines they rode to the event. They stripped the street gear, such as lights or even brakes, and after they had competed, they bolted the gear back on and rode home. The idea was it gave the ordinary enthusiast a fair way to compete with his peers, which was why the bikes were strictly production, as delivered by the factory. The rules even required the rider to be the owner, with papers to prove it.

Back in the early 1930s, there was only one notable dealer who sold imported (read: English) motorcycles. Reg Pink had a dealership in the Bronx, and he knew that the most important thing a dealer could supply was something for his customers to do with their motorcycles. Pink knew that early in the twentieth century, when the spoilsport English government banned racing on public roads, the tourist-friendly chaps on the Isle of Man invited racers to compete on their lovely island.

The Eight-Valve race engine displaced 61 cubic inches and could propel bike and rider to speeds of about 120 miles per hour.

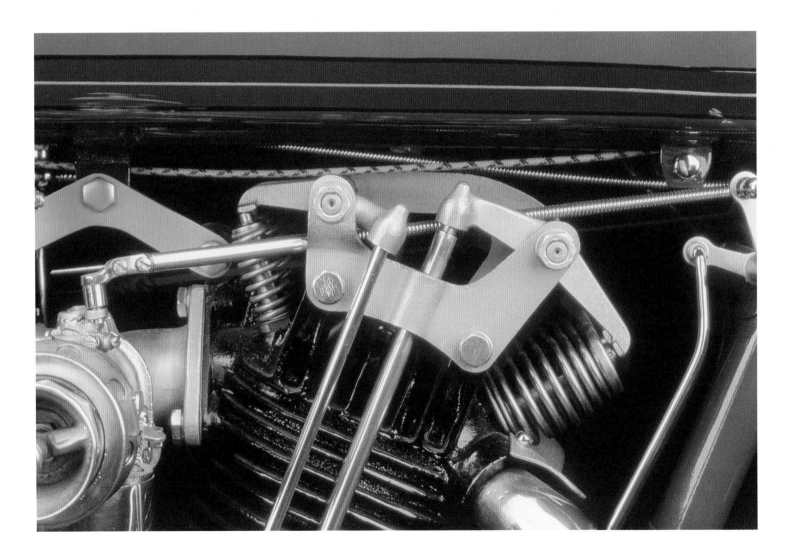

The invitation was accepted. The top event at the Isle of Man was the Tourist Trophy, quickly shortened to TT.

One Sunday afternoon, Pink went into the country, borrowed some land, and laid out a course in the dirt, over hills so steep you could jump into the air. It seemed (to him, anyway) like a miniature replica of those Isle of Man laps, so he called the event the TT.

An Indian executive and top guy in the AMA came to watch Pink's TT. He was intrigued and wrote an article for the AMA magazine explaining the new event and its rules. Presto! TT became a uniquely American off-road event.

At the time, the AMA's competition committee realized that the pure racing classes were dying out. The crowds weren't big enough to pay the kind of prize money that would allow professional racers to buy or maintain their machines. As a potential cure, the AMA devised a national championship for Class C.

If two valves per cylinder can make good horsepower, think what four valves will do! That was the thought process by Harley's engineers in 1916, which led to the Eight-Valve racer. This is a 1923 model.

BACKYARD MECHANICS MADE TT MODIFICATIONS TO THEIR BIKES, AND EVENTUALLY THOSE MODIFICATIONS LED TO BOB JOBS, OR BOBBERS, WHICH LATER EVOLVED INTO CHOPPERS.

In 1938, Sam Arena raced the Harley-Davidson 45-cubic inch WR to a 200-mile record-breaking time. It proved to be a wonderful racing motorcycle.

In the early 1930s, both Harley-Davidson and Indian made 750cc side-valve V-twins that were marketed as sportbikes, so the rules for the new Class C events required the motorcycles to be side-valve 750s. Because Pink was a valued member of the AMA and his customers' sporting mounts were overhead-valve 500cc singles, such machines were also allowed in Class C. At the time, this equivalency formula was one of inclusion, rather than exclusion, and it provided fair competition (as well as heaps of politicking, as we'll see in due course) for nearly thirty years.

The first Class C Nationals were held in 1934; Harley-Davidson had the only factory Class A team. That team consisted of one rider, Joe Petrali, and Petrali won every Class A title in the 1935 season, which turned out to be the last year of Class A racing.

In 1934, Harley built a competition version of its basic 45-cubic-inch model and marketed the bike to people who wanted to race. Many riders bought the racer, rode to the races, stripped the road gear, and raced against riders mounted on Indian Scouts. The new Class C regulations were a success. Class C did in fact save the sport of motorcycling in the United States. New talent showed up, and guys (along with some women, notably Dot Robinson, a top enduro rider) bought what they raced and raced what they bought. Class C was truly the national class by 1939.

In addition to the 45-inch class, Class C featured an open class that allowed any engine size. It turned out that the Model E, the legendary Knucklehead introduced in 1936, did very well in TT events. Owners began modifying the Big Twins, removing the front fenders, moving the Big Twins, moving the back fender to the front, and raising the bars so the rider could stand over the jumps.

There were kits to raise the engine in the frame, for more ground clearance, and the exhaust pipes ran down the side of the bike, at exhaust port level, to keep the pipes from being crushed on jumps or drowned in water crossings.

Backyard mechanics made TT modifications to their bikes, and eventually those modifications led to bob jobs, or bobbers, which later evolved into choppers. Choppers evolved into customs, which evolved into today's cruisers. The current Softail Deuce can trace the origins of its stylish good looks straight back to Depression-era TT racing. The fashions of the 1970s, which became the sales force of the 1990s, began as the production racer of the 1930s.

THE WR

Class C revived racing and many new events sprang up, most notably the road races at Daytona Beach, Florida.

This was another one of those happy accidents. Daytona's beach—actually the event began at Ormond Beach, the next town to the north—was a God-given, hard-packed surface used for speed runs. When race cars got too fast, the locals came up with a race for stock cars. The cars raced up the beach and down the narrow asphalt road parallel to the beach for 200 miles. The first race didn't make 200 miles, however, because race organizers hadn't reckoned on the tide coming in.

When the motorcycle road races at Savannah, Georgia, were canceled, the AMA was invited to race at Daytona Beach. This event had serious sales potential.

Harley and Indian both tested the limits of the Class C principle, Indian by the straightforward production of a limited number—fifty, according to the official records—

Board-track and dirt-track racers
such as this 1924 FHAC Harley
had no transmission, only direct
drive to transfer power to the rear
wheel—and there were no brakes!

Many enthusiasts don't realize it, but Harley's twin-cam concept dates back to the mid-1920s. This 1926 FHAC board-track racer's engine is an example of that early twin-cam design.

of racing machines known as "Big-Base" Scouts because of their strengthened crankcase. Harley-Davidson was subtler. In 1941, the same year the Scouts arrived for Daytona, H-D introduced the WR.

There were two models. The WR and WRTT. According to Motor Company press releases, the WR models were simply Ws without lights, mufflers, brakes, and all the other gear the racers removed. Why make the customer pay for stuff he'll throw away?

In reality, the WR and the WRTT were both a lot different from the W or the WLD, or even each other, than they looked.

The WR, made for flag ovals, came with what was known as the light frame, made of stronger steel than the WL's frame. The WR had no brakes, and a WR was at least 100 pounds lighter than the WLDR.

The WRTT was intended for heavier TT duty, which included jumps and deep ruts. It used a trimmed version of the WL frame with extra bracing, although in 1948, the factory switched to a braced version of the light WR frame.

ABOVE: Sidecar race, July 4, 1921.

LEFT: Willard "Red" Bryan on Two-Cam OHV, circa 1929.

The FHAO's specially built engine was cradled within its frame, using stout steel plates to reinforce the spindly tubing.

The WR engine had the same bore and stroke and outward appearance, but inside the flywheels were steel instead of iron. The camshafts were radically timed and a magneto handled ignition chores rather than points and coil. The cylinders also differed, with the valves closer to the bore, and with the valves tipped toward the piston, to aid combustion chamber flow. The area between valves and piston was sculpted and massaged, also for better flow.

The ownership rule was still in effect, but somehow WR cases often left the factory without numbers, to be added later, or in multiples, so the "owner" (actually a dealer or tuner) could have several engines but only one title.

Both models were available with numerous options. The standard WR and WRTT used saddle tanks slung over the frame's top tube, gas and oil side by side. But for the longer road and dirt events, there was an optional pair of gas-only tanks, with an added oil tank beneath the seat. There was a long list of sprocket and gear choices, and the rear hubs could be fitted with two sprockets, so if the inside of the tire wore, the wheel could be flipped for a fresh section of tread.

The factory revived the Racing Department and hired a racing engineer but didn't hire riders. Instead, the engineer worked with the engineers in the production division and

ABOVE: Most records suggest that fewer than fifty FHAOs, or Eight-Valve Racers, were made from 1916 through 1928. This is 1927 model has a girder-style fork.

LEFT: A single side-draft carburetor protruded defiantly from the right side and into the airstream to feed the 61-cubic-inch Eight-Valve engine.

with the dealers who sponsored teams and with the outside tuners, several of whom knew as much as the factory.

There was sort of a pyramid—the sponsored rider without backing, equipped with a WR and a WRTT and all the options, had an edge on the WR rider with one machine, who, in turn, had an advantage over the guy who had stripped his WLDR.

But there were riders whose talent put them ahead of the riders with equipment, and the Harley faction was pretty much equal during this time to the Indian backers and the Norton, Matchless, and Triumph contingents, who won at least their share, considering they were always outnumbered.

The bottom line is that the sport of motorcycle racing survived the Depression. There was a pause during World War II, of course, but after the war, when prosperity came roaring back, racing picked right back up, with hardly a pause. With the WR, Harley-Davidson had made another in its history of smart moves.

THE KR: FORWARD . . . AND BACKWARD

As soon as the Allies' victory became a matter of when and not if, Harley executives began planning for the future. In their usual cautious manner, H-D introduced the little Model S, the 125cc two-stroke single aimed at the youth and entry markets, but the really

ABOVE: Hillclimbing was high on Harley's race agenda too. Unlike board-track racers, the hillclimbers had high handlebars, giving the riders additional leverage necessary for navigating uphill.

OPPOSITE: This 1930 JD-based hillclimber relied on its chain-wrapped rear tire for traction during each ascent.

One of the direct results of the AMA instituting Class C racing was bikes like this 1936 Harley-Davidson RLDR.

new bikes didn't arrive until 1952. Even then, new was relative. The new street machine was the Model K, a unit engine with unit-construction crankcase and gearbox, hand clutch, foot shift, and rear suspension that kept pace with the wildly expanded import market.

With the K came the KR and the KRTT. These were nearly direct descendents of the W, the WR, and the WRTT. At first glance, the KR and KRTT looked like the street-going K minus road gear.

Again, not so. While the flathead K engine shared its bore, stroke, and 750cc displacement with the KR, the R version used low-friction ball and roller bearings. The K had needle bearings and bushings. The KR's valves were tipped toward the bore, like the WR's and the camshaft timing was radically different. The ignition was magneto rather than the K's generator.

The KR frame featured no rear suspension. The KRTT used a swingarm that pivoted at the rear engine mount and had shock absorbers bolted to the swingarm at the bottom and the rear of the frame at the top.

There was a third model in the Competition Department book, albeit seldom seen in the showroom or in real life. This was the KRM, designed for racing in the western deserts. The KRM had a skimpy muffler and front fender and used roller main bearings, which lived longer, but otherwise was like the KRTT.

ABOVE: Al "Squibb" Henrich at St. Louis hillclimb, 1932.

RIGHT: Al Nelson (kneeling), Daytona Beach, 1940.

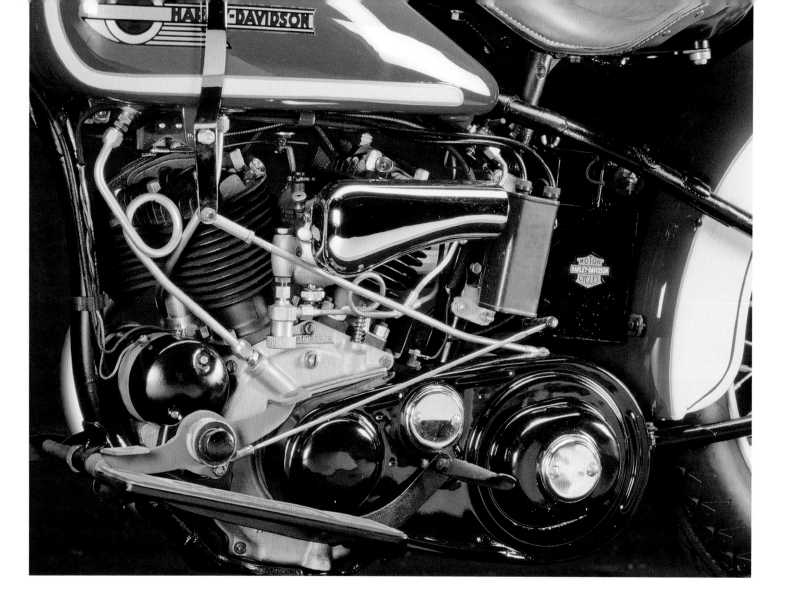

The left side of the 45-cubic-inch RLDR engine shows off a clean carburetor air horn and the bike's tank-mounted hand-shifter.

The AMA's national championship rules changed in 1954. Previously the AMA awarded the No. 1 plate to the winner at the Springfield, Illinois, mile. For 1954, the AMA devised a series that included short-track, half-mile, mile, TT, and road-course events, with points awarded at each event and the championship awarded to the rider with the most points.

By the early 1960s, imports had made major inroads, and the AMA again changed the rules, with short-track nationals contested by 250cc production-based engines, modified and placed in special frames.

In another of these happy accidents, Harley-Davidson had replaced the homegrown two-stroke singles, the Hummers and kin, with four-strokes from Aermacchi, an Italian maker absorbed into H-D.

The Aermacchis—named Springs for the US market—provided the engines for the CRTT and CRS racers. The road-racing CRTT featured a tuned engine in a lightened stock frame modified with rear-set controls, clip-on handlebars, and a choice of tanks and brakes. In 1963, the AMA allowed full fairings in the road-racing classes. The CR, the short-track model, featured a lighter and lower frame, and lacked brakes and lights.

AN ERA ENDS

There's no question these machines, the KR and KRTT especially, were successful racers. But racing doesn't stand any stiller than life, and as the 1960s closed, there was more and more proof that the old side-valve KR and the production-based C-series Sprints were on their way out.

Gary Nixon won the AMA title for Triumph in 1967 and 1968. Mert Lawwill restored the No. 1 plate to the Harley camp in 1969, but Gene Romero won for Triumph in 1970 and Dick Mann for BSA in 1971. Then came the two-strokes. Yamaha had a 350cc two-stroke twin that was perfect for modification, and the little 350 became a match on the road courses for the big 750 side-valves and 500 overhead-valve singles. The AMA's competition committee, comprising racers and promoters as well as factory reps, was aware of all of this, and in 1968, they changed the Class C and AMA championship rules.

The production requirement remained, with 200 examples needed, although the machines need not be street legal. And there was simply a 750cc limit, with valve location and number of cylinders free choice. The new rules were to apply to dirt track in 1969 and road racing in 1970. This set in motion a series of circumstances that led to the side-valve KR's last great achievements. The rule change came at a bad time for Harley-Davidson. The Motor Company was in deep financial trouble, about to be taken into the American Machine and Foundry conglomerate. In the long run, AMF kept H-D alive, but in the short run there was no money for a new, or at least up-to-date, racing program. When the 1969 season opened, Triumph and Gary Nixon came loaded for Milwaukee's Finest, with a Triumph twin and a triple, both of which were 750cc overhead-valve engines producing more power than the side-valve KR ever dreamed.

Nixon lost the National to H-D's Fred Nix, on a KR, and Harley's Cal Rayborn—arguably the best road racing talent of his or any era—won the 1968 Daytona 200 on a KRTT Lowboy, so called because the KRTT frame was lowered and wrapped around the engine, all tucked inside a full fairing.

But in 1969, the final version of the KRTT, featuring two carbs, a full fairing, and huge brakes, was inexplicably slower in qualifying than it had been the year before.

On race day, it rained. One week later, having used the providential time to sort out the last two carbs, Rayborn won again. He won by outlasting the Yamahas, which were much faster. It doesn't say "Lucky Break" on the trophy, but something clearly had to be done.

THE NEW ERA BEGINS . . . BADLY

When the new rules were announced, team boss Dick O'Brien and engineer Peter Zylstra knew they were in for a tough time. There wasn't much time, and there was less money to come up with a competitive race bike. For inspiration, they went back to 1958, when the new XL Sportster got an unpublicized teammate, the XLR. This was mostly an XL top end, but with hotter camshafts and bigger valves, atop KR cases with the ball and roller bearings from that racing engine. The XLR was built for national TT races, which at the time allowed overhead valves.

The XLR was a competitive TT mount, so when the Racing Department needed a new 750cc racer, the engineers shortened the XLR's stroke, revised the camshafts to suit the displacement and timing, and put the engine in a mildly reworked version of the KRTT frame. The new model was named the XR-750. It was a beautiful motorcycle, as clean and crisp as any racer ever made. And it was a disaster. The XL engine used cast-iron for the cylinders and heads, while the big Harley twins had used aluminum heads since 1948. The XLR raced TT, which required short bursts of power followed by braking and turning, while the mile and half-mile course kept the power on all the time. The iron retained heat and the engine melted, earning the XR-750 the nickname "The Waffle Iron."

Poised and ready to go, this 1948 WR is ready to hit the dirt on an oval-shaped track. The racer weighed about 300 pounds and had no brakes.

Displacement for the S-series 125cc two-stroke single was upped to 165cc in 1953. This mid-1960s short-track racer is powered by the 165cc version.

As the rules required, the factory assembled 200 XR-750s and offered them for sale. There was a separate run of XR-750s for road racing, with revised Lowboy frames and bodywork. The equipment appeared in the 1970 catalog as the "Road Race Group."

The road racers debuted at Dayton and promptly blew up. The 1970 season was a debacle. The team and racing department did some incredible and extensive work on the Ironhead XR, all to no avail. Factory records show approximately 100 1970 XR-750s sold, with the leftovers dismantled and put back in the Parts Department, or spirited out of the factory.

The iron XR had one heroic occasion. Late in 1971, the H-D team was invited to a series of road races in England. The team's alloy XRs weren't ready and the brass didn't want to look bad, but Cal Rayborn wanted to go. Walt Faulk, an H-D employee, had built his own iron XR engine, so he and Rayborn went off to England.

They're still a legend there. Faulk somehow kept the fragile engine alive just long enough to finish each race—the cold English weather didn't hurt—and Rayborn rode the wheels off the bike. He won three of the six races and came in second in the other three. Say "XR" to an English fan to this day, and he'll say, "like Calvin rode."

THE ALLOY XR

If there was a good side to the Waffle Iron's failure, it's that O'Brien and Zylstra and the team had a chance to do a lot of research. It paid off. For the 1972 season, with AMF willing to invest in the product, the team introduced another XR-750. This time it was done right, with alloy heads and barrels, twin carburetors, and an absolutely up-to-date racing engine, still in the classic 45-degree V-twin.

The alloy XR began with as much power as the hand-grenade iron XR had in its final form. Then, the alloy XR got better. Also thanks to AMF, the team could hire riders, the top men. In the dirt, the alloy XR was king. Mark Brelsford won the AMA title in 1972.

Then the racing world changed. Yamaha's 350 two-stroke twins were competitive and its 650 four-stroke street conversion was almost as good as an XR-750 in the dirt. For road courses, Yamaha built the TX700, a full-race 700cc two-stroke with all the brakes and streamlining that it needed. Yamaha shipped enough of them to the United States to qualify for Class C racing, and Kenny Roberts Sr. won the AMA championship in 1973 and 1974.

KR racers dominated Class C racing from the late 1950s through the 1960s. The straight exhaust pipes on this 1966 model produced a loud, bellowing sound.

THE GNC BECAME A BATTLE OF RIDERS AND TUNERS, EVERYONE BEGINNING WITH THE SAME PARTS AND RULES, AND THE XR-750, LIKE THE OFFENHAUSER INDY ENGINE AND THE COSWORTH V-8 IN FORMULA ONE, DOMINATED ITS CLASS FOR A GENERATION.

The four-stroke twins built by the Yanks and the Brits weren't competitive with the two-stroke fours from Yamaha or the two-stroke triples from Kawasaki. Harley-Davidson's road-racing XRTT faded away. The team used the model for several seasons and took part in some European races, but Harley's team was never again a factor in AMA road racing.

THE NEW LIGHTWEIGHTS

Aermacchi had been involved in racing long before H-D absorbed the company. The Italians went through the same painful learning experience at the hands of Yamaha and responded with two-stroke twins of their own, in 250cc and 350cc versions.

The machines attracted top talent, notably Walter Villa, who rode the water-cooled twins to the world 250 title in 1974, 1975, and 1976. Villa also won the 350 title in 1974. The 1974 championship was Harley-Davidson's first world title.

The AMA had a road-race class for 250s, so Harley homologated the Aermacchi as the RR-250. In its debut, the RR-250 piloted by Gary Scott beat Yamaha's national and later world champion Kenny Roberts. But it never happened again, and because the 250 class was the junior class and didn't count toward the national championship, the RR-250 faded away.

Aermacchi's imported Sprint 250 was the basis for Harley-Davidson's entry into short-track racing.

Aermacchi and Harley tried the Yamaha approach, doubling the 250 Twin into a 500cc four, but it was too complex and too far from what H-D was actually selling to customers to justify the expense.

Next came a 500cc twin, a radically enlarged version of the RR-250, and designated (what else?) the RR-500. The RR-500 had lots of power. Gary Scott, who won the AMA No. 1 plate for Harley in 1975, rode the RR-500 in Europe but spun out in the rain. The Harley team went to the AMA national at Laguna Seca and was in the hunt when a clamp loosened. Scott retired and the Harley never raced RR-500 again. Why not? Scott and O'Brien agreed that the RR-500 wasn't competitive and that the money and time needed to make it so would be better spent on the XR-750. Which it was.

THE XR RULES

By the late 1970s, the XR-750 was the best motorcycle in dirt-track racing (which evolved into a separate series from road racing), so much so that the English teams withdrew. The alloy XR-750 was truly a production motorcycle, for racing if not for road use. The first 200 sold out, so in 1975 the factory built another 100 dirt models. There were also 50 frames made for road racing in 1972, with lower steering heads and frame backbones wrapped

The single-cylinder, four-stroke Sprint engine displaced 250cc. Its low-slung engine helped make it easy to maneuver on oval dirt tracks.

ABOVE: Throughout the 1950s Milwaukee dealer Bill Knuth (left) remained a sponsor of Class C racing. Here Knuth stands next to two KR and one WR flat-track competition specials.

RIGHT: Although the K engine proved dominant on the track, helping riders like Everett Brashear win races all across America, it proved less successful on show room floors. Here Brashear receives a trophy from Jim Davis in 1955.

around the engine. There was another run in 1976 and 1977, and 200 more came off the production line in 1980. Since then, there have been other production runs at the foundry.

Nature fills vacuums, and Honda and Yamaha returned to the Grand National Championship (GNC, as the AMA shorthands it) in 1981, both with stupendously reworked versions of their road-going V-twins.

Neither worked. But while Yamaha quit losers and retired from battle, Honda bought an XR-750, took it home, dismantled it, and asked themselves, "What would Harley-Davidson have done, if Harley-Davidson had our money?" Then, they did it. The RS750 featured an overhead-cam engine with four valves per cylinder. Honda had built a better Harley. Honda went on to win the AMA title with Ricky Graham in 1984, and with Bubba Shobert in 1985, 1986, and 1987.

The AMA decided that because there were a couple hundred Harleys and a handful of Hondas and the Honda had the better engine, the racing wasn't fair. So the Honda engines were restricted, evening out the power difference. Harley's Scott Parker won the GNC title in 1988.

Honda withdrew from dirt track and the XR-750 has been the winning machine ever since.

A new era for Harley-Davidson racing began in 1970 when the XR750 was introduced. The first model was powered by a modified Sportster engine.

ABOVE: By 1972, Harley-Davidson had developed the all-new alloy XR750 engine. This design is among the most successful race engines in history and remains competitive today.

RIGHT: Although the alloy XR750 engine resembles the road-going Sportster in appearance, it is an entirely different design.

ON THE ROAD RACE . . . AGAIN

When Yamaha's two-stroke four took over the road races on the AMA circuit, the fans lost interest. In 1983, race promoters tried to revive fan interest by inventing a new series: The Battle of the Twins. At that same time, H-D introduced the XR-1000, a Sportster with a version of the XR-750's two-carb top end. O'Brien and the racing shop took some old XRTT parts, converted an XR-750 engine into an XR-1000, put Jay Springsteen on board, and won the race going away. Those who were there still remember the look on the leading Ducati rider's face when Springsteen caught him in the corner, pulled even, then motored away.

The team handed the equipment over to a factory-backed privateer, Harley dealer Don Tilley, and with help from the Harley Owner's Group, Tilley and rider Gene Church ruled The Battle of the Twins series for the next three years. It wasn't exactly a major series, nor was the machine—named *Lucifer's Hammer* by O'Brien, a Harley racer in the tradition of the WR or the KR—but it did make the H-D fans happy and it did fill the grandstand at Daytona.

Meanwhile, there were changes inside the GNC and out. The AMA dropped the 250cc limit for short track and mandated 500cc singles for that class as well as the TT class. Harley-Davidson didn't make a big deal, but there was no problem. H-D simply arranged for Rotax, the Austrian engine maker, to sell racing engines through Harley dealers.

LUCIFER'S HAMMER AND A NEW ERA

By 1986, the AMA had made another set of changes. In response to public taste, the Superbike class had been expanded, eventually eclipsing the two-stroke class, known as Formula One. The Japanese focused on road racing, and the AMA's GNC was left to Harley-Davidson.

As a result, the GNC became a battle of riders and tuners, everyone beginning with the same parts and rules, and the XR-750, like the Offenhauser Indy engine and the Cosworth V-8 in Formula One, dominated its class for a generation. Still, there was plenty of competition, even if the XR-750 was the only competitive mount, and there was constant improvement to the engine. But times changed. For the 2002 season, the AMA admitted certain motorcycles with 1,000cc overhead-cam engines and the 1,200cc overhead-valve engines into the GNC, provided they were fitted with devices to restrict their power output.

That new formula helped bikes such as the 1,200cc Buell and Suzuki's TL1000, which featured a 1,000cc V-twin engine, to equal the mighty XR-750 in power output. Or so the theory went. Having put his XR-750 at the front of the pack for 2001 to win his third career GNC title, Chris Carr and his XR-750 remained in the catbird seat the next four years, earning the No. 1 plate from 2001 to 2005, also tying Parker's AMA record of five straight GNC titles (1994–1998). This wasn't the first time that Carr managed to rain on Parker's parade, though. He happened to be the rider to break Parker's five-year grip on the coveted plate in 1999. But by the end of his career, Carr scored *only* seven GNC titles to Parker's record nine. Both riders wore Harley team leathers during their combined sixteen years of GNC domination and, of course, both riders scored most of their wins riding the famous XR-750 as well.

Meanwhile, tuners for those new non-Harley hybrid Class C engines were making headway in terms of power and speed for their bikes, until eventually the XR-750 wasn't necessarily the dominant bike anymore. Oh, it still won races and championships, and the

THE TEAM'S ALLOY XRs WEREN'T READY AND THE BRASS DIDN'T WANT TO LOOK BAD, BUT CAL RAYBORN WANTED TO GO.

The Aermacchi-based CRTT road
racer was successful on America's
tracks during the early 1960s, but
eventually the faster Japanese
two-strokes proved superior.

most notable XR-750 rider to win during the first fifteen years into the new millennium is Jared Mees, scoring GNC titles in 2009, '12, and '14, plus he was joined by Harley teammate Brad Baker who took top honors for 2013.

The Class C hybrid engines finally gained a foothold in being competitive on America's dirt ovals thanks to more power and speed, and for the first time in many years the GNC became a battleground for more than one brand, although it remained clear that the XR-750 was still the bike to beat if a rider wanted to have the inside track for winning the AMA's coveted No. 1 plate.

V-ROD PRO STOCK

But the real show for Harley-Davidson's racing program as the new century got underway was taking place on the NHRA (National Hot Rod Association) quarter-mile drag strips of America, where a team headed by a couple of legends were—as drag racers like to say—putting the competition on the trailer. The two legends were Terry Vance and Byron Hines, the majordomos behind the Vance & Hines company logo and former NHRA Pro Stock champions themselves. Well, let's back up a bit and say that Vance and Hines and their Harley-based drag team were learning to put the competition on the trailer because in drag racing, as in any racing, first-place trophies usually take a while to come by, and the new Screamin' Eagle/Vance & Hines pro stock drag racing team had a lot to learn

The fairing on this 1972 CRTT road racer helped the formidable bike slice through the air at speeds of about 120 miles per hour.

QUALIFYING FOR THE FIRST 2005 RACE, TONGLET SET THE QUICKEST QUALIFYING TIME IN NHRA PRO STOCK BIKE HISTORY WITH A 7,007-SECOND PASS AT GAINESVILLE.

when their first rider, GT Tonglet, went to the starting line for his first-ever pass in 2002 aboard his V-Rod-based pro stocker.

The saga began shortly after Harley-Davidson parked its ill-fated VR1000 road race program for good. Nature abhors a vacuum, and there remained a huge vacuum in the Motor Company's race plans, so Harley-Davidson signed Vance & Hines (both the men and their company) to spearhead a new NHRA Pro Stock drag racing team. The Pro Stock program was all-new territory for Harley, and making matters even more complicated, the race effort was centered around the all-new V-Rod 60-degree V-twin engine that was unlike any Harley engine before (well, with the exception of the VR1000, and even Harley management said both engines share the same pedigree, although no single part from one can be swapped for the other, so we'll just stick to the racetrack facts for now).

NHRA rules at the time permitted two-cylinder V-twin engines larger displacement compared to their four-cylinder counterparts. But usually in racing there's a catch, and in this case the caveat was that the large V-twin engines must use pushrods to activate the intake and exhaust valves, and that's where Byron Hines played a key role in prepping the dual-overhead-cam V-Rod engine for the competitive pro stock class. By cleverly incorporating tiny pushrods into the liquid-cooled engine's design, Vance & Hines magically made the new V-Rod eligible for NHRA Pro Stock competition.

The team's first two seasons proved to be steep on the learning curve. Throughout the 2002 season, the single-rider team failed to qualify for a single elimination bracket, meaning that Tonglet never got to race head to head with another rider all season. Things improved for 2003 and Tonglet even managed to be top qualifier at the Mile-High Nationals at Bandimere Speedway near Denver, Colorado. And, as if the folks in Harley's front office were affirming the team's progress, late in the season a young man named Andrew Hines—yes, another member of father Bryon's family that includes his older son and former three-time NHRA Pro Stock champion Matt Hines and the fledging Screamin' Eagle–sponsored team's crew chief—signed on as Tonglet's teammate.

But neither Harley rider scored a win in 2003, which also happened to be the Harley-Davidson Motor Company's 100th anniversary year. The pro stock team's first win would happen in 2004, and in a big way when the message was sent loud and clear during the season opener at Gainesville, Florida. There the two Harley-mates fought their way through the elimination bracket to the final round, which guaranteed that Harley-Davidson would score its first-ever Top Eliminator award too. Hines won that historic showdown—well, actually it was more of an intramural race—becoming the first man to win in NHRA Pro Stock aboard a Harley-Davidson.

The success at Gainesville set the stage for the remainder of the 2004 season until finally Hines joined his father and brother as an NHRA Pro Stock champion. The Screamin' Eagle/Vance & Hines bikes proved so dominating during the 2004 season that, in hopes of leveling the Pro Stock playing field for 2005, the NHRA handicapped the Harleys with 40-pound weight ballast, setting minimum weight at 615 pounds compared to 575 pounds for the rest of the field.

"Adding 40 pounds to our bikes on such short notice was a demanding situation," said Byron Hines. "I sat our riders down and told them they were really going to have to step it up while we worked hard to make up for the extra weight."

Both riders answered the call, and their top speeds and elapsed times—the benchmark to measure success for drag racers—didn't reflect the added weight at all.

Fact is, just the opposite held true. Qualifying for the first 2005 race, Tonglet set the quickest qualifying time in NHRA Pro Stock Bike history with a 7.007-second pass at Gainesville. But stop the clock: almost immediately Hines answered that with the first-ever sub-7-second ET, posting a 6.991-second qualifying run. Two ET records in back-to-back passes. Maybe more weight was necessary after all if the competition was to be given a chance.

But the NHRA was steadfast in keeping the weight handicap at 40 pounds for the time being, and the Screamin' Eagle/Vance & Hines team remained steadfast in steamrolling the competition, scoring win after win. By season's end the younger Hines notched his second consecutive NHRA Pro Stock championship, and Tonglet had enough points for runner-up. That's a tough act to follow for 2006.

Variations of Harley's RR250 (and RR350) road racer were responsible for several FIM World Championships for factory rider Walter Villa.

The pro stock team responded in a big way for 2006 and Hines made it three NHRA Pro Stock championships in a row, tying a record that was shared by his older brother Matt and one of the top female pro stock racers ever, Angelle Sampey. And for 2007 Eddie Krawiec became Hines's new teammate. The following season Krawiec responded, winning what was to be the first of his three NHRA Pro Stock titles aboard the Screamin' Eagle/Vance & Hines bike (2011 and 2012).

After a two-year dry spell, Harley pro stock team came back to dominate the NHRA competition for 2014. In the process, Hines recorded his fourth pro stock title, making it seven team championships in thirteen seasons of racing.

Harley's association with Vance & Hines extended beyond the end of the quarter-mile drag strip, though. Taking a page from Europe's playbook, Harley-Davidson and Vance & Hines created a co-op in 2007 that led to the formation of the AMA Vance & Hines XR1200 Series, which amounted to a spec class of road racing for the venerable Sportster, in this case the new-for-2007 XR1200.

The goal behind the XR1200 Series was to provide a road race championship that was affordable for Harley dealers to partake in and be competitive. That's precisely what happened too, and the racing couldn't have been closer. For several years, the AMA Vance & Hines XR1200 Series served up-close, competitive racing, but the XR1200 itself lasted only a few years in Harley's lineup, so eventually everybody—the AMA, Harley-Davidson, and Vance & Hines—elected to call it quits with the XR Series.

A pair of protruding air filters help to identify the formidable XR750 flat-track racer.

Regardless, racing, in one form or another, will probably always be a part of Harley's corporate fabric. Oh, there's no doubt that, as time goes by, the racing itself will change. That's the way it's always been because progress leads to change no matter how you look at any situation. Especially in racing.

But the orange, black, and white team colors will continue to be seen at racetracks across America because that's what Harley-Davidson chooses to do—race. As Dick O'Brien, Harley's legendary race boss during the 1960s and '70s, once said, "Harley-Davidson races because it gives our customers a place to ride to on their bikes." Perhaps a simplification of why the Motor Company races, but OB's words pretty much hit the mark, because racing has a lot to do with tradition.

In the words of another, and more recent, Harley team boss, Bob Farchione, "Racing continues to be one of the most important aspects of what we do at Harley-Davidson. Motorcycle racing is part of our tradition and history." It's a tradition and history that one of the company's founding fathers, Walter Davidson, instilled into the corporation's DNA way back in 1908 when he put Model 4 at the front of the pack to register a perfect score in the first-ever enduro he ever entered.

Although the VR1000 never won an AMA Superbike race, the bike's progressive design helped lead to the V-Rod in 2002 as a production road bike.

INDEX